6/11/73

Civilization, the Next Stage

Also by Bruce Allsopp

NOVELS

Possessed
The Naked Flame
To Kill a King

HISTORY

A General History of Architecture
A History of Renaissance Architecture
Decoration and Furniture—The English Tradition
Historic Architecture of Newcastle upon Tyne
The Great Tradition of Western Architecture
(*In collaboration with H. W. Booton and Ursula Clark*)

AESTHETICS AND CRITICISM

Art and the Nature of Architecture
Style in the Visual Arts
The Future of the Arts
Architecture

DESIGN

Decoration and Furniture—Principles of Modern Design

ORIEL GUIDES
(*In collaboration with Ursula Clark*)

Architecture of France
Architecture of Italy
Architecture of England
Photography for Tourists

VERSE

The Loving Limpet
(*under pseudonym, Simon Grindle*)

Civilization, the Next Stage

THE IMPORTANCE OF INDIVIDUALS IN THE MODERN WORLD

by

Bruce Allsopp

ORIEL PRESS LIMITED

First printed in Great Britain, 1969

SBN (69 UK) 85362 061 x
Library of Congress Catalog Card Number 75-80755

Published by Oriel Press Limited
at 27 Ridley Place, Newcastle upon Tyne
Text set in 11 on 13 point Baskerville
Printed in Great Britain by
Northumberland Press Limited, Gateshead

CONTENTS

v

PREFACE

A GOOD reason for writing is to find out for oneself. This book started as an exploration seventeen years ago and has several times been completely rewritten as my experience developed. In the summer of 1968 I felt that a point had been reached at which it was possible to distil the years of study and thinking into a book about the increasingly urgent predicament of mankind which is manifest in the current loss of morale, confidence, sense of direction and faith in the value of life or indeed in any values.

I make no apology for my artistic bias[34] because politicians, economists, technologists, faceless organizations and others have made a sorry mess of things in losing sight of the art of living and the conditions of happiness.

I have tried to produce, in essential form, an argument about and an attitude towards life, as it is now, in order to indicate attainable goals for humanity beyond those envisaged in the social and moral philosophies which still dominate our ways of thinking.

No man can be 'qualified' to write such a book as this: indeed any of the directly related academic disciplines would almost certainly inhibit the attempt! But the need to see life whole again is urgent and that is what I have tried to do. I have made it as simple as possible, so that it may be accessible to many people, but there is a limit to simplicity in the expression of difficult matters. The book is therefore less easy to read than I would wish but as clear as I can make it, and I hope that any academic reader whose territory I cross will not regard as facile passages which have in fact been exceedingly difficult to simplify and condense.

I owe a debt to many people with whom I have discussed sections of the work, with or without their being aware of what was going on, and others who have helped in various ways. I hope the book will be of value but it could not, by the nature of the subject, have achieved completeness. A good deal has been pruned during the final revision and may be incorporated in a second volume.

Stocksfield.
February, 1969.

Chapter One

THE CHALLENGE TO LIVE

THIS BOOK is written in the belief that life is worth living, that the human species is on the whole pleasant, that it is capable of improving in quality and that it has the possibility of a future. Man's future is not assured: he will have to continue to prove himself worthy to survive, and we can be reasonably optimistic. In the prevailing current of thought and feeling this is a sufficiently unusual statement to make it seem necessary to begin by recognizing the nature of the challenge which faces mankind and causes some people to despair.

Men had to live in communities to survive; they had to be enterprising to prosper; they had to have weapons to hunt and to protect themselves; they had to be acquisitive to raise their standard of living above brutish levels; they had to believe in gods to explain themselves to themselves. Communism, capitalism, militarism, materialism and religion are all basic to primitive human nature and each has proved capable of developing from a support of the individual man into a system which crushes him. What is beneficial on a small scale can, and frequently does, become its own opposite merely by increase in size. (A dose of medicine can cure, an overdose can kill.) This applies to humanity itself and following the invention of disinfectants and antibiotics our fertility, resulting in the population explosion, changes the birth of a child so that, though it may still be an occasion of joy to the parents it is also an incident in a sinister process of destruction of

1

mankind by increase. Consequently it is very hard to sustain belief in the sanctity, privilege and individual value of human life when we can see the progressive diminution of human stature to the point where we may become like maggots or locusts in our abundance, a world *infested* with men. There is enormous irony in the fact that, by concentrating upon prosperity and welfare, we are preparing the destruction of our material standards, threatening the viability of communal existence, nullifying the possibility of enterprise, stultifying belief in ourselves and entertaining the ghastly possibility that war, with killing on a vast scale, may seem to be the only method, short of natural disaster or divine intervention, by which the biological clock may be put back to a point where we can try again to achieve the good life.

More than three-quarters of the earth's population is sunk in ignorance, illiteracy and squalid fertility sustained by the medical bounty of the scientifically advanced minority. More than three-quarters of men and women lack sufficient education to think validly about the problems of modern life and only a tiny fraction, even in the advanced countries, have minds sufficiently cultivated to sustain the technological basis of our kind of civilization beyond the level of dial-watching, switch-pressing and routine maintenance. If a few thousand creative and educated minds were to be eliminated (the so-called *boffins* of this world), as could so easily happen under a government actuated by mass ignorance, millions of human beings would die of starvation and disease. This process would almost inevitably be assisted by war. The danger is acute. We have reached a decisive point in human evolution. If we take the right decisions there is a good prospect of man being able to live in much better ways; but if we fail, the work of the last five thousand years will all have to be done again differently, or, like so many of nature's experiments, be written off for ever.

This book is concerned with the urgent problem of living and governance in the modern world. All the systems we know are weighed in the balance of human experience and found wanting. There is no *system* which will work and we have to go back to the individual man. The great illusion is that by corporate systems we can solve the personal problems of living. These can only be solved by individual people and in terms of individuality. We have to go back to simple but difficult questions like *What is life about? What are we for? What is worth while?* and *Why are we here?*

In our time, just when we thought we might have achieved a sensible, humane way of living, not for a privileged few but, at least within some national frontiers, for people in general, we are faced with total failure, with the agonizing truth that we have achieved so little that we are in danger of believing we have achieved nothing. It is a crisis of confidence in ourselves.

The fundamental error is the belief that social and political systems of one sort or another can solve man's problem of living but the absurdity of this idea can be seen if we imagine the conditions which would exist if one political system, let us say the American or the Russian—it scarcely matters which—were to triumph. As in all conflicts (notably the two world wars of 1914-18 and 1939-45), the winner would approach much nearer to the loser's position, in order to obtain victory, and in the end there would be a world state which it would be impossible to govern on the principles of either of the contestants, because each exists by virtue of opposition to the other and neither offers a way of life which inspires respect. The existence of a world state would create a political and ideological vacuum and, being relieved of the challenge of opposition, men would be forced, at last, to face the essential problems of living. This would produce a rapid disintegration of the world state, as conceived by present standards, which are national standards of competitive power writ large. Remove the competition and the logic of power would disappear. This is why science-fiction so often escapes into the fantasy of wars and competition with other peoples in space, because we realize sub-consciously that though we are cherishing a nonsense we do not know how to live without it. A world state would have to be disintegrated into regions, each working out its own way according to its climate, geography, economy, traditions, aspirations, quality and races and this would mean that at last we should have to face the realities of man living on a small sphere in space.

But having failed to face these realities, these fundamental problems, because we have been preoccupied with other and obsolete problems, we have reached a point of crisis at which, possibly by warfare with thermonuclear bombs and biological horrors, possibly by the increase of population to the point at which civilized life becomes impossible, but more likely by our simple failure to create conditions of self-governance under which it is possible to preserve confidence in the value of living, we may fail as a species. There is no guarantee that man is nature's final answer. If we perish, as other species have perished, this is not the end of the world. We need to come to terms with our own cosmic insignificance and yet prove that we are still capable of evolving into something better. Nothing in the universe 'stays put' so far as we know.

It is our privilege or misfortune, according to how one looks at these things, to live at a point in time and evolution when man as such stands on trial. And it is to man as such that we must look for an answer, not to systems but to the quality of men and the quality of living. We have conducted, especially in Britain, an elaborate and wonderful experiment which has proved in terms of the low quality of living achieved, that the improvement of material conditions is not enough.

It is true that we could go a great deal further in improving the conditions of living but we have gone far enough to see that the creature we are dealing with, man, *ourselves*, is selfish, rather stupid and *under developed*. It is with this selfish and stupid creature, with his fears and superstitions, his false loyalties, his prejudices, his love, his courage, his splendour, his weakness and his unfulfilled potentialities that we have to deal. Systems have their uses but they have proved their inadequacy to cope with our condition. We are forced back upon the individual, upon his beliefs and his behaviour, because the systems are but a reflection of these. Utopias notoriously break down upon human nature and it is a mistake to believe that human nature is fixed for all time. It is with human nature itself that we must be concerned if we are to survive this present crisis in the evolution of *homo,* presumptiously called *sapiens.* You only need to translate it into English to see how silly the name is *'man the wise'*; clever, yes—clever Dick—but wise? Oh dear, no.

It is valuable in any situation to consider the next step if we succeed in what we are doing now. We already have an awareness of the need to abolish armed conflict between states and powers. If we were to succeed in achieving a world polity in which, for example, no state had the power to make war and all subscribed to a police force which existed to stop the use of force (not necessarily the best answer) the present systems and ideologies which are considered worth fighting for would lose most of their relevance and a vast amount of resources, mental and material, would be released for creating better ways of living. Have we any idea what those ways might be? Much of our dissatisfaction is due to the fact that we have not sufficiently considered what kind of life we would want to have if we could; and yet it is clear that many of us are sick of the present struggles and the bankruptcy of social and political thought and action throughout the world. We are like children who have been brought up in a lunatic asylum and are suddenly asked what we want to be when we grow up. We don't know what sort of a world it is outside.

Men may be conditioned to fit systems or systems may be made to serve men. If system triumphs over humanity we shall achieve a way of life like the ant hill or the bee hive.

('Go to the ant—he is there for a warning.') If the system is to serve man, man must know what he wants to be, how he wants to live and, most important, what he wants to strive to become, because our present ways of life are messy, ugly and unsatisfactory. Man is only on the fringe of achieving what it is conceivable he might achieve in quality of living. If we believe this, if we believe that as a species we have a great deal more to do and a long way to go, that there is still a cause to work for, and that cause is the destiny of man himself, then we must pick our way through the sludge of accumulated prejudice and ignorance, cruelty and corrupt morality, superstition and stupidity in order to discover faith in ourselves. This may be achieved by finding out, in terms of modern knowledge, the truth about ourselves.

If we have lost faith or confidence in ourselves it is largely because we know that a great deal of the political, social, moral and religious apparatus upon which former faith rested is unsound, corrupt and untrue. *One cannot have faith in what one does not believe and one can only believe in what one believes to be true.* This is so obvious that it needs to be stated. Much of this book must be very simple because the problems are so complicated. It will be an exploration, not a final answer and it will seek to achieve the lucid brevity of a gospel not the cautious prolixity of an academic thesis.

It is a peculiarity of our age that, whereas in other times, throughout man's history, it has been difficult to survive, in our day it is difficult to live. Despite our manifold problems the advantage is with us. But the old challenge to endure, to suffer the consequences of ignorance, violence and the overwhelming load of discord with fortitude, are being replaced by challenges which require quite different kinds of response. A large proportion of babies stand a good chance of having an adult life. Relationships between and among human beings can be expected to endure for years. Yet the habits of thought formed under other conditions, the conventions and the values necessary for men who lived in much greater peril than we do, remain as a barrier to the evolution of new and fuller ways of living.

A feature of our time is preoccupation with the imminence of disaster, with the destruction of mankind by the consequences of war. It would be foolish to ignore this possibility, but perhaps we tend to cherish our fear because it helps us to believe that we are not different from our ancestors, and this fear which we cling to is itself a principal cause of the danger of war. Our fear also encourages us to retain the old standards of courage, faith and resignation which were high virtues. Our fear can be our excuse for not living. Despite the very real danger of overpopulation, which most people flaccidly ignore, our fear is no longer predominantly of famine and disease, of grinding poverty and the hardships of exceedingly crude social and economic patterns. We are, more than any men have ever been, in possession of the means to create security and prosperity. We have much of the knowledge and many of the skills. We have fantastic resources of power and apparently limitless capacity for research and invention, yet it is often said, and possibly with truth, that there is less, not more, happiness than there was in times when odds against us were very much greater.

Our new conditions of life, which offer us opportunities and pleasures beyond the wildest dreams of our forebears, present us with a challenge which is perhaps more subtle and more difficult to face than unknown countries beyond civilized frontiers or, at home, the daily weight of difficult living with very long hours of toil and the ever present incomprehensible threat of early death. There is still unpleasant toil, there are still poverty, disease, accident, and localized war but the balance has shifted. The old ethic was made up of fortitude, resignation and courageous pioneering (which we cherish in our love of 'Westerns' and our adulation of astronauts). The challenge now is not to recreate the old values but to welcome new opportunities and make new values such as our ancestors could only conceive vaguely as possibly existing in heaven.

Our fear is now of ourselves. Psychology has helped us to see the measure of our own nature. Sociology has helped us to understand that the relationship of society to the individual and the individual to society are problems not to be solved by inherited tribal customs fossilized into moral codes. Technology has given us immense power; philosophy has made us think about the nature of our existence; physics has presented us to ourselves as minute specks in a universe of unknowable size, and art has turned away from representation to the revelation of new kinds of experience. Even in the garden there are flowers which never existed before.

Given almost limitless opportunity we lack, or think we lack, happiness. Given a fairer prospect than ever man had before, we become cynical, unproductive and preoccupied with sordid things. Given a challenge to live abundantly we falter. Given the chance to escape from a dark old morality we giggle uneasily.

It is no longer any use to call the people back, like strayed sheep, into the old folds of conventional piety nor does any system of political or social organization stand up to the questioning of honest men. There is no panacea, no simple remedy which will put things right easily, but this book is written in the belief that there is a splendid future for mankind if men choose to make it. It does not offer a religion nor a system of belief but it does try to look at the nature of life and of man with the hopefulness and faith which have made men keep on for some two hundred thousand years.

It is not a book for cowards, for those who expect life to be easy and lay themselves open to discouragement. In the long evolution of man such people have not mattered. And among all species inability to adapt has been the prelude to death. The people who really matter are those who try.

Chapter Two

A BASIS OF TRUTH

THE MOST important revelation of science is that we are
born into a world which is reasonable and consistent wherever we are able to study and understand it. This is an
astonishing fact of which nearly all our ancestors, up to the
beginning of the twentieth century, were unaware. The
universe is not constructed in an arbitrary and capriciously
inconsistent manner: wherever we are able to investigate, it
obeys laws which are understandable by us as logical. If we
purge ourselves of prejudice and superstition we find that
our minds are capable of apprehending the way the universe
works as though it were designed by someone like ourselves.
This does not prove there is a god but it does mean that
our way of thinking, the apparatus of brain cells and acquired
scientific learning, is consistent with everything else. There
are laws of nature given not devised. It is reassuring to find
that the world is rational. Our ancestors believed that it
was subject to the activities of alien and irrational spirits,
acting arbitrarily and capriciously instead of according to
divine logic as revealed by modern mathematics.

The term 'divine logic' must not be misunderstood. I use
the term *divine*, not to imply the existence of a god but in its
accepted meaning of 'superhumanly excellent' (OED). It has
been said that 'God is a mathematician' but I only wish to
state that mathematical laws exist and are valid as far as
the most powerful telescope can penetrate.

On Earth, and probably elsewhere in the universe, life came into existence. It happened a very long time ago but not so long ago as what we can see happening in distant parts of the universe.

Our modern awareness of the vast size of the universe gives us a false sense of insignificance. There is no reason to believe that either size or duration are important. What, indeed, do we mean by *important?* It may be a nonsense question. Importance is a value-judgment and we may suspect that a value-judgment implies the existence of a judge. Is there such a thing as a cosmic judge? If not, then the importance of anything may only be relevant to the situation in which it exists or happens.

In the past value-judgments have generally had a foundation of religious belief and the character of the belief had a profound effect upon the way of life of the people who held the belief. If, for example, they believed, as many people have done, that this life was a 'vale of tears' through which one went as a sieve and preparation for a better after-life, there was an incentive to believe that only those things— such as prayer or chastity—which contributed to expectation of the good life after death were really valuable. There was a tendency to shelve the problems of a better life on Earth and to believe that suffering and self-denial here might even be a qualification for special happiness beyond the grave. Though the influence of this system of religious belief has been enormous, and in many ways beneficial, very few people have taken it so far as actually to welcome death, which would have been the logical conclusion. This failure of logic can be explained by saying that the flesh is weak, and man has to struggle with the weakness of 'the flesh' in order to achieve salvation: thus arose the extraordinary concept of there being a distinction between body and soul amounting to the existence, in each human being, of two persons—one of the flesh and the other of the spirit. The flesh is condemned to death but the soul, as it is called, survives in heaven. This is all part of a splendid hypothesis about the nature of man.

There are many other systems of religious belief but it would be inappropriate to discuss them here at this stage. The point is that *any* system of belief or faith can be a basis for value-judgments about what is worth while and what is not worth while in life and, by extension, what is right and what is wrong. Religions can answer the question 'what is the purpose of life', and from religion we have come to *expect* an answer to this question. We *assume* that there is a purpose, but we do not easily accept, in the modern climate of thought and knowledge, the implication of our assumption and of the word *purpose*. We assume that there must be a purpose and become quite neurotic if we cannot see what it is, without realizing that the existence of a purpose really implies someone who purposes. Either *purpose*, that is to say *what is intended for us* is generated within ourselves or outside ourselves. We may be dissatisfied (most people are) with our own justification for ourselves, with being an end in ourselves; but if we expect a purpose, an intention about us, from somewhere outside, it is difficult to see how this can exist unless there is some super-human power which intends for us, in other words, a god.

We want to start with open minds, so let us face the fact that for at least five thousand years nearly all men, until very recently, believed in a god or gods. They did not necessarily believe these gods were good. The ancient Greeks thought their gods were unkind and capricious: they were superior, immortal beings whom men had to try to persuade and please by means of burnt offerings which the gods were supposed to like.

So long as men believe in gods the question 'What is the purpose of life?' can always be pushed off on to the gods. And if someone asks *'What is the purpose of gods?'* the answer is that we don't know, and it does not matter very much because we have to live under them, like a subject people under a conqueror. What the gods are *for* is the gods' business, not ours.

For the last two thousand years in Christendom men have believed in a *good* God. This was a concept which grew, mainly through the teaching of Jesus, out of the older idea which the Jews had of Jehovah who was not always good. His principal advantage over 'other gods' (*Exodus 20, 3.*) was that he was on the side of the Israelites.

Men have conceived God in very many different ways, sometimes as a super-man, sometimes as a mother, sometimes as a spirit—the Holy Ghost for example—but, whatever the form, God or the gods had intentions for man and, throughout the ages, man has come to rely on this. Now if we ask what the purpose of life is we are keeping the idea of a purposer, that is to say of a god. If we do believe in God the question is meaningful, but if we do not believe in God it may well be nonsensical. The question is loaded and we cannot honestly begin by asking what may be the purpose of life. It will be better to start with life itself, as we know it, and try to understand its nature. This might be called starting at the bottom and working up, rather than beginning at the top with assumptions we cannot prove and then working down, as man has generally done.

Chapter Three

WHAT ARE WE?

SCIENCE HAS not answered this question. It can describe and classify us: it can to a large extent explain the processes by which our species came into being and developed to the present state of man: it can elucidate the mechanism of heredity and birth; but it cannot say what we *are* in any meaningful way.

It seems that under certain conditions matter can come alive. It is then life in an extremely simple and minute form but it is capable, during an immense period of time (by our standards) of developing. The conditions which favour the emergence of life happened on Earth and there is no reason to suppose that they have not happened elsewhere. But if life has come into being on another planet different conditions of atmosphere, gravity, climate and chemistry are likely to have produced quite different creatures from those which inhabit, or have inhabited Earth. As *Man* we probably are unique in the universe, simply because the long series of accidents and adaptations over millions of years has involved such a vast number of chances and choices, leading up to Man, that it is almost impossible that exactly the same series can have occurred elsewhere, despite the enormous extent of the universe. But there is every reason to suppose that if life does exist elsewhere it evolves according to the same physical laws which apply here. If life is 'a phenomenon of matter' there may be other phenomena about which we know nothing. Life seems to imply the existence of a body of some kind but many phenomena of matter can exist without anything we would call a body—electricity for example. Very simple experiments will show that a particle of dust can have a charge of electricity which will affect its movement in relation to other particles. The Earth is prevented from falling into the sun, or disappearing out of range of the sun, by forces which we cannot see but which scientists have studied. We know that in a battery the positive terminal and negative terminal must exist, and the idea of the existence of positive and negative throughout the structure of the universe is a platitude of modern physics, but only to a certain extent understood. We do not know how far the principle of a negative counterpart for a positive may go. There might, for example, be a negative (or positive) counterpart for each of ourselves. We do not know, and we should accept that there is a great deal we do not know, but as far as we can understand, anything which exists or happens in the universe does so in conformity with what we call physical laws which are consistent. This does not mean that everything the physicists say is right—there is a great deal they don't know and when more is known some supposed laws may be modified *to conform with the facts*. The faith of the scientist is that the world is rational and nothing has emerged so far to prove this faith wrong. Without it science as we understand it could not exist. If things happen which seem to contradict reason then they need very careful study to find out firstly whether they happen and, if they do, what was *wrong* with our previous reasoning.

These are difficult matters and the point of alluding to them here is to make clear that life is a phenomenon of the physical world and it can and should be studied rationally. But there may be other phenomena of the physical world which we do not know about, or have never studied rationally, so we should not rule out as impossible the existence of a soul associated with a body like a charge of electricity in a dust particle. It is not impossible, nor is it irrational, to believe that there is some kind of directing unseen force, such as one might expect primitive people to call a god, existing purposively in the world, perhaps limited to the solar system, as man probably is to Earth, but possibly permeating the whole universe. We just do not know. It is unscientific to dismiss the evidence there is in generations of human belief and we do seem to need new techniques for considering the possibilities of soul and divinity scientifically. So far practically nothing has been done along these lines and it must be said that religion has not encouraged the rational examination of its foundations.

Man is probably a unique phenomenon. He exists in continuity by continual renewal in the process of birth. We know that each birth involves a rearrangement of genes from mother and father so that a new unique creature, related but different, comes into being. It is true, but rather unfashionable to admit, that the child is a creation, an extension of the flesh of its father and mother. This used to be called a blood relationship but is not: it is a *gene* relationship but the old idea was not so very wide of the mark as to make much practical difference.

The child is thought of as being younger than its parents but genetically, and in terms of the evolution of the race, it is older—having one more generation behind it and being one generation further along the evolutionary ladder. It is also possible that it may embody some mutation which makes it 'better' in some way than its parents or, conversely, it may have started off an abortive experiment in evolution. With its physical equipment genetically one generation older— that is to say more developed—it acquires, through up-bringing and learning, the experience of yet one more human generation, that of its parents. Considered in this light there is little to be said for the domineering, self-righteous father figure and it is only natural that the parent-child relationship is frequently difficult. It is a wise father who finds he can learn from his children.

When one is born one comes into being as a separate self conscious creature. The reason why one is born is a sexual act by one's mother and father which may have been undertaken deliberately to produce a baby, but even if it was so planned the desire was for *a* baby not for the particular self-conscious personality which has just emerged from the body of its mother.

In the womb the baby depends for sustenance upon its mother's blood—which may be different in kind from its own—and at birth its food becomes milk without which it cannot survive. Its first consciousness of separation, of selfhood, seems to be painful and it cries. It cannot survive by itself. If the mother dies or cannot look after it the new human being is dependent upon others without whose succour it will inevitably die. For some years its dependence is such that it cannot live without the care and support of older human beings. This rearing period is long by comparison with other creatures. The human child is forced by dependence into an extensive period of supervision and instruction which makes possible the passing of accumulated experience from one generation to another. This is one reason for the superiority of man over other animals.

The child has no reason to be grateful for the act by which it was conceived because, as a person, it did not exist, and even if it was imagined it was not wanted for its own benefit. But as soon as the child is born it becomes involved in a net of personal relationships from which it can only escape by death, or a deliberate act of withdrawal which is more and more difficult to arrange in a crowded world. On the face of it there is no obligation upon the parents to rear the child. In some societies it has been the practice to inspect the baby and if it was unsatisfactory to let it die. A bitch with a litter of puppies will lick them over and if she does not like one of them she may discard it, though she becomes a devoted mother to the others. Not all mothers want or like their babies but with the great majority there is a tenderness which

cares for the little human being and, despite all the inconveniences, the mess, the lack of sleep, the savage and demanding nature of the creature, manages to love it and give to it.
We begin our lives in debt, not for being conceived but for
being pitied, nurtured and even loved.

In our society infanticide is illegal and this has, perhaps,
the unfortunate result of concentrating attention and responsibility upon the sexual act, from which conception is a
possible but by no means certain result, instead of upon the
prolonged and deliberated act of nurturing the child, which
is a legal obligation. It has long been fashionable to shrug off
one's parents by saying 'I did not ask to be born', even
to indulge in self-pity if one knows one was not wanted. It
would be more logical, at least, to say that the unwanted
child owed the greater debt to its parents for nurture. It is
also worth noting that hardly any child comes up to its
parents' expectation. This is partly the fault of our way of
continuing the human race by insisting that mutual sexual
desire is the proper prelude to parenthood irrespective of
any genetic faults which there may be on either side. Probably the basic instinct of girls to get themselves pregnant
by heroes is much sounder than possessive males care to
admit, and the desire of a healthy male for a physically
beautiful mate is likewise eugenic. Of course there are risks:
heroes can be bogus and beauty can be devoid of brains or
compassion.

The conventions of our society are such that the unwanted
and rejected child is cared for by the community through
homes or foster parents. Even the imbecile and the deformed
are nurtured with care and allowed to breed when their
season comes. This morbid and frightening state of affairs
arises, in some people's thinking, from Christianity, but more
commonly from fear of the consequences of entrusting
powers of decision about the life of a baby to any human
agency, though we are less scrupulous about terminating the
lives of certain criminals or of military enemies and we con-

stantly risk lives, our own and other peoples', in many of our activities.

These matters will be discussed at greater length later and are only touched upon here to indicate the curiousness of the state of human thinking which surrounds the baby when it arrives. In the highly irrational environment, conditioned by innumerable taboos based upon mistaken interpretations of nature and prejudices induced by social conditions which no longer exist, the baby depends upon other people. Thus at the beginning of life it is barely self-conscious and entirely dependent; and as it grows up it becomes more and more aware of itself as a personality and at the same time, whether it likes it or not, more enmeshed in the complex of human relationships like a cogwheel in a gear box.

If we now return to the question at the head of this chapter, *What are we?* the answer could be, for each and every one of us, something like this:

'*I am a temporary arrangement of matter which derives directly, over millions of years, from a primitive organism by a long series of genetic incidents occasionally modified by mutation. The last in the series was the union of my mother and father and out of millions of possible arrangements of their genes, all of which might have produced someone different from me, and with about even chances that it might have been a person of different sex, I came into existence by being born from my mother's body. Since then I have been brought up and educated, partly according to a plan but quite largely by accident, and I have acquired a great deal of knowledge and some skills of mind and hand and my tastes have been conditioned by the environment, human and physical, which I have experienced. I am therefore, a typical human, not quite the same as any other. I belong to a community in which I have been brought up (or into which I have migrated) and I am dependent to a large extent upon the goodwill and work of other members of that com-*

munity with whom I have common interests. In short, I am a unique being but I am linked genetically to my ancestors, socially to the community and educationally to my parents and the people among whom I was reared.

'Do I have a soul? *It is a very important and interesting question. I do not know the answer but religion teaches that I have, and psychologists think of my personality as being divided, if I may over-simplify, into (a) what is basic equipment, inherited and acquired, and (b) what I do about it. The big unanswered question is what does I mean. Certainly something unique but equally certainly part of something continuous. The continuity may be through my fertility or through what I think and do, or in both of these ways. What I do falls into two main categories, my work and actions and my relationships with other people.'*

These two things, actions and relationships, form the subject matter of most of the rest of this book.

Chapter Four

SEX AND POPULATION

THE CONTINUITY of man, as of all creatures, depends upon sex and wherever we look in nature we can see evidence of enormous over-insurance for survival. A picturesque way of looking at this is to say that Nature (whom we tend to think of as some kind of organizing female personality) has arranged sex so that survival may be ensured even under the most adverse conditions of famine, war or pestilence. Seed is produced in vast quantities, not only by plants but by man. A less romantic but probably more accurate assessment is that, in the long process of evolution, only those species have been able to survive which were fertile. Creatures which were fierce and strong probably had less need to be fertile than those which were easy prey. Man was fierce but not very strong and therefore doubly vulnerable. He is equipped with a very powerful sexual urge and produces a great quantity of seed most of which is surplus and goes to waste.

Throughout man's history fertility (which was often worshipped as divine in ancient times) has only just been able to maintain a slow increase in human population and there have been periods when communities have died out. Man, as part of nature, shared in the primal urge to continue his species and, until now, the encouragement of people to have children was always desirable and sometimes vital for communal survival.

Having used his brains to devise weapons man made himself more formidable than even the strongest lions and tigers, but he also used his armaments in competition with other men and war became an apparently permanent factor in human existence. To survive, a community had to breed, not only for replacement of natural loss by old age, accident and disease, but also to increase its strength in fighting men.

There have probably been men on Earth for about 200,000 years. It has been estimated that it took 199,000 years for the world population to reach 300 million which implies a tiny growth rate of only 1,500 a year. By 1830 there were about 1,000 million people on earth. By 1930 there were 2,000 million and now we approach 4,000 million. In many parts of the world half the population is less than 18 years of age and their reproductive potential is terrifying. Man has never before had to cope with such a population explosion but it has happened in animal communities and the observed results have been 'the development of low fertility associated with a great variety of physiological and behaviour abnormalities'.[1] In man this would mean the growth of apathy, neuroses, perversions, and drug addiction. This seems to be happening. So it is clear that in our time the relationship of sex to our way of life is changed, abundant fertility is no longer a benefit but a threat. An excess of good has become an evil.

If no natural restraint comes upon population growth, then the prospect before humanity is one of degradation, increasing squalor and eventual starvation, but long before this the ruthless competitive survival-urge in men would have led certain communities to destroy others in order to make room. Something like this has happened before on a very small scale in the barbarian invasions of the Roman empire, when peoples of the sparsely fertile lands of central Asia overflowed and initiated what we call the Dark Ages. Our present condition is infinitely more menacing and armed with weapons which are so powerful that they might sterilize the whole of Earth and turn it into a lifeless desert. There is nothing unnatural about a planet with no life on it and looked at from a cosmic point of view, if we imagine some thoughtful creature observing Earth from afar he would conclude that a form of life had emerged, developed for some millions of years and then extinguished itself. Just that.

This can seem to be a very gloomy background for Jack and Jill falling in love, but there is a brighter side. Love can be 'a many splendoured thing' but a high proportion of the misery in the world has been caused by sexual problems and the morality which surrounds them. If we have to look at this entirely afresh it is no bad thing. The first stage has been a loosening of taboos and restraints, what has been called a more permissive attitude to sex. This is not enough.

Sex is a powerful and ruthless instinct for using our procreative organs to beget children but it was only at a relatively recent stage in human development that men realized there was a connection between intercourse and child-bearing. With animals there is no awareness of future consequences. The instinct is blind and the incentive is pleasure. The sensation of pleasure is enhanced by the relief of pressure, emotional and physical. The word naturally associated with sexual intercourse is *satisfaction*. This is short-lived, as one might expect, because nature is prodigal of seed and over-insures the survival of the species. It is in the very nature of sex that it should only give sufficient satisfaction to make it worth while and the appetite grows by what it feeds on, just as other human faculties tend to be developed by using them, whether they be of mind or muscle.

The pursuit of sexual satisfaction is like chasing your hat down an endless wind tunnel. The only finality is exhaustion for the simple reason that, in terms of crude nature, we are built and equipped to procreate. We do not even have seasons, as animals do, but are sexually active all the year round until we wear out. This is not a basis for civilized life in which a birthrate of more than three children per couple is a disaster signal. Sex is something we have to come to terms with, and they have to be terms of our own making not those suggested by the sexual physiology of our bodies.

In the past man has tried, and to a large extent succeeded, in coming to terms with sex in the context of the conditions in which he lived. When men lived by agriculture they were well aware of good strains and bad strains in breeding animals and not unreasonably they applied the principles of good husbandry to their own breeding and the morals associated with it. Thus, for example, in Jewish law, a man was not allowed intercourse with a slave girl for forty days after he had bought her.[2]

Sex is regulated by a complicated glandular system in the body and there are, in fact, many degrees of masculinity or femininity on either side of the hermaphrodite (that is the human who has the attributes of both sexes).[3] A change of sex is also possible and not very uncommon. People can properly be described as being 'more or less male or female'. They are all *human* and this fact needs emphasis because the sexual distinction is not nearly so important as it is usually made out to be, except for its primary purpose of getting babies.

The secretions which govern our sexuality affect our character and behaviour in ways that one might expect, bearing in mind the natural function of sex to continue the race at all costs. The female is adapted to nursing the child and the male is activated to provide for his family. The motivation of most people is, quite naturally, the bringing up of a family and the most difficult time in their lives may be when the menopause terminates a woman's fertility and a still virile husband is subjected to the ethical constraints of a society in which only one wife at a time is allowed. It is at this stage, not surprisingly, that men sublimate the sexual urge by work for work's sake, or committees, or become aggressive and intolerant, or otherwise try to adjust and sometimes fail.

In the male, energy and enterprise are apparently partly a byproduct of his sexuality and an important part of the art of living is to learn to channel a primitive urge, which was necessary for a cave man, into the activities of modern life. Mankind has long experience of this. The basic motivation may still be wife, family and home, but, being intelligent, man learns to come to terms with the conditions of doing a job. Furthermore, an aspect of sex is display for admiration. This is common throughout nature and man is no exception. His powers of physical display are limited compared with, say, the peacock, but an important part of his courting ritual is display of his prowess, originally in fighting, like a cock robin, but latterly in sport and in work which is reflected in his income and the standard of comfort he can offer his bride. Men get into habits of work and achievement which outlast their sexual justification. This is just as well.

It is not easy for humans to be quite honest about their own sexuality but it is something we have in common with animals and birds whose instincts and behaviour are like our own. An important part of their sex life is nest-building or home-making. Sex is the underlying motive for this and we likewise are activated to make homes, places in which to live with our mate and rear our children. It is part of sex-life. In thinking about sex we should take into account all its aspects and not just the act of copulation, as so many people tend to do in thinking about sex. In fact, insofar as we are animals, the meaning of life is to be found in the sexual cycle of birth, rearing, adolescence, courting (including in the case of the male, proving his capacity to support a family) mating, home-making, giving birth, rearing children, taking the responsibilities of an elder and accepting the limitations of old age and then dying. When we talk about sex life it is this rounded whole that we should consider. Most sensible people do in practice but our morality is distorted by falsely emphasizing part of it out of the context of the whole.

But man considers himself different from the animals and there is good reason for this. His claim to distinction is founded upon what he is and what he does, over and above being an animal. Many men, especially in the middle ages, have despised and tried to reject their animal nature. To some extent this has proved possible but the ascetic can only exist in a minority capacity and sustained by a majority of people who accept the sex life-cycle. In terms of modern popular democratic attitudes there is a tendency to reject the idea of an élite to whom the development of man as man is entrusted and we prefer the concept which is perhaps most clearly expressed in the phrase, 'that of God in every man'[4] (whether we understand what we mean by God or not. This will be discussed later). Meanwhile we must note that man as man-different-from-the-animals is something over and above the self-justifying phenomenon of life. It must be something which man himself generates by the quality and creativity of his living. The question must therefore arise, and indeed does arise in the experience of most thinking people, what relationship is there to be between the sex-life of man and the humane structure which he builds upon it, over and above being an animal?

In practice it is a problem which has to be resolved, as far as it can be resolved, within the personality of each individual, but just as we don't have to start digging a garden by making our own spade so, in matters of this kind, we need tools to work with. These tools are provided by conventions, customs, recorded experience, morals and laws all of which may, like any other tools, be imperfect. In devising and using such tools we need to see clearly what the tools are for. The spade is for digging. The tools we need are those which will enable us, as individuals, to live with our physical nature and the instincts which are built into it. We must be on our guard against tools which have the quite different purpose of enforcing a pattern of life which other people approve, *regardless* of the potentialities of our own individual natures.

Chapter Five

THE IDEA OF SELF AND THE PROBLEM OF DECISION

PSYCHOLOGY HAS helped us to be more sensible about sex but we have, at the present time probably over-compensated and given it too much importance. Animals are not entirely slaves of the life-cycle. Birds appear to sing for pleasure and animals play for the fun of playing. A castrated animal is not noticably miserable and we may waste our pity on the gelding or the neutered cat. Conformity to the biological life cycle, the blind fertility discipline of nature, is by no means the criterion of an enjoyable life. Indeed the reverse is true and fertility commonly goes with squalor. To say that a spinster is a 'failed woman' is to give a completely unjustified weight to biology and it is obviously at variance with observed performance. Many spinsters achieve a quality of living which is enviable. A physical handicap, such as sterility, is not necessarily a barrier to living happily. Furthermore, nature herself seems to breed people with different degrees of sexuality. The abnormalities, such as homosexuality, are not un-natural: they are a natural occurrence just as much as normalities. It would be very unwise to say that the unusual is also the unnatural.

In recognizing that our sex-life is motivational, necessary and basic we must avoid the inversion of logic which might justify giving it a dominant role over our human nature. We are not even the kind of animal that is naturally and firmly faithful to one mate; and even in our sex-life a considerable degree of supervision by ourselves, as human beings, over ourselves as animals, is essential for the achievement of behaviour which is acceptable in any human community.

The concept of a human self which is over and above the physical animal entity called a man is very difficult to explain. It is hard to understand how something can exist which is completely dependent upon the physical body for its existence, and to some extent at the mercy of the physical body for its 'character', and yet is separate. Both psychology and religion have had to accept such an idea, a distinction between body and spirit in the case of religion and the identification of a super-ego in the case of psychology. As we move from a mechanical age to a greater dependence upon and understanding of electronics it becomes easier to conceive a kind of existence which is a 'charge upon' or 'field around' another, but the idea of a self as something which does exist, at least partly distinct from the physical body, remains a working hypothesis which we do not fully understand, though it is necessary as a way of *thinking* about what we do actually experience. For many centuries this self, or soul, or spirit, whether or not it survives death, has been regarded as the essential human being and the body as the vehicle. We still have to make the distinction to think about ourselves as we know ourselves to be—able to decide within limits what we will do.

Our experience of ourselves is that we are unique, and this is corroborated by the science of genetics. Each of us is a unique combination of biological elements programmed by the unique genetic pattern which occurs, apparently by chance, at conception. We know ourselves as a body which has its own demands, disciplines and limits and as something else which depends upon the body but exercises some authority over it. Mostly we regard this something as being the real self and to us, at least, it is important. We refer to it as ME.[5]

The idea of *me* as something important not only to myself

is very old. It is expressed in the religious idea that all souls
are equally important to God. That was one way of thinking about it but psychology has helped us to clarify our
understanding of this. At the risk of some over-simplification
the position may be stated like this.

'*We now understand that there is a basic, given nature,
like a hand of cards dealt in a game; but there is another
part of ourselves which can play this hand well or badly. I
probably cannot alter my basic nature but there is a part
of me which can control and develop what is given, cultivate
is so that it will grow like a plant, bear flowers of some sort,
and perhaps seed. Every decision I take affects what I am.
For example, I cannot give myself a better brain than I was
born with but I have the choice, all the time, between making
the most of it, encouraging it to grow, or just letting it lie
fallow. I can try to make the best of myself, which means
effort, or I can be lazy and not develop what I have to the
limit of its capacity.*

'*Though I cannot make myself very clever if I am not
clever, or become a great musician if I am not built that
way, I can do a great deal to make the best of what I have.*'

This is not an entirely new idea though its development
as a psychological insight is modern and it presents a challenge to modern people which men and women in former
times did not recognize. They believed much more in fate
and destiny, as we see in the ancient Greek plays and even
as late as Shakespeare.

'*I can myself decide what sort of person I want to be. I
can be dishonest, tricky, unreliable, unkind and unpleasant
to other people or I may set myself standards of unselfishness
and devote myself to helping people who are less fortunate
than I am. These are decisions which I can take, whatever
my basic equipment.*'

It is only fair to note that Christianity has always taught
that a man is in charge of himself and can, at any stage, reject
what he has been (repent) and start to rebuild himself. (This

teaching by Jesus was one of the great forward leaps in human thought.) Obviously, if one has gone a long way in a wrong direction it will be a long way back, but not an impossible journey. Christian thought did not, however, seem to be able to compass the idea of forwardly creating oneself as distinct from repairing the ravages of sin by repentance. There is a glimpse of the idea in putting one's trust in God and obeying his laws, but as long as men believed in supernatural and irrational (that is to say inconsistent) forces, such as God and fate operating ambiguously and arbitrarily outside the laws of nature, it was perhaps inconceivable that man can make himself by a linked series of choices which are conditioned by his basic make-up (program if you prefer to think in computer terms) and the interaction of this with his environment. Most of the choices are made instinctively or in ignorance. Some are mistaken and some are fatal. Man is not captain of a ship which he is steering on a known course to a defined destination but modern psychology, though it uses different terms, has tended to confirm the old belief that man is in charge of his own soul and, as a person, he can to some extent steer the organism which carries his personality and in the process actually develop his personality.

'What sort of people do they think we are?'[6] is a famous question which implies that we have an idea ourselves of what sort of people we are. Our nature is complicated and hard to understand but we can now think of a basic 'given' nature and a superior nature which is able to decide what to do with what is 'given'.

What we do decide is affected by what we admire. What we admire is affected by the quality of our thinking, by the extent of our knowledge, by ideals, by reading, by standards and by the condition in which we keep our body. In other words, quite simply by what we recognize as being good or bad, better or worse and what we do about it.

There is a tendency to admire people because of their cleverness, talent, intelligence or physical qualities such as strength or beauty. It might be better to admire what people make of what they have been given. Here again, we should note that Jesus took this view and the idea that God, who knows all the facts, is the only one who should 'judge' is a way of saying this.

Inevitably we have reached a point at which the words *good* and *bad* must be used. Even if we accept the ideal Christian view, that judgment is with God and only God may judge human beings, we ourselves still have to make ethical decisions about what is the right and what is the wrong thing for *us* to do. Our lives involve a long chain of decisions, many of them trivial, like 'shall I taste the beef or the potato first'. Some decisions are easy and unimportant but others are like Y junctions in a road—go left and you get to one place, go right and you get to another. Even if you turn back there is a significant difference that you arrive at a different time, and such a time difference can be very important for your future life. Healthy people make most of the minor decisions of living very easily and often unconsciously but some decisions are difficult. We ask ourselves what is the *right* thing to do and what is the *wrong* thing to do? The answer is sometimes very difficult to give.

One way of coping with the difficulty is to 'pass the buck' in a variety of ways such as consulting an oracle, studying the stars or simply tossing a coin. The underlying superstition is that some external force will decide what is best to do. Another way is to try, by prayer for example, to open one's soul to God who will give guidance, and a variation on this theme, is to trust one's conscience which is conceived as being a built-in moral compass or a 'still small voice' which is always right. (There is, however, some danger that one may mistake the voice of self-interest for the voice of God.)[7] Another method is to accept the dictates of some code which lays down what is right and what is wrong. This can cover many common situations but obviously cases occur where the law does not seem to apply clearly and anyway, what is the basic justification for the law? Another method is to apply reason to the problem and argue what is the right thing to do, but reason is often unable to provide an adequate answer because you have to begin by establishing values. For example, a surgeon has to choose between saving the life of a mother or her child. It may be impossible to make this decision without making or accepting value judgments.

On the face of it decisions about good and evil are so difficult for sophisticated modern people that there is a strong temptation to say that good and evil are just a matter of opinion. But this is not enough. We do need some kind of framework within which to make decisions because a great many of the decisions we make do have effects upon ourselves, upon other people and upon the limited surface of Earth where we live. It is possible to break the problem down while recognizing that some decisions will remain very difficult. Difficulty is not an excuse for abdication.

Man is a decision-making animal. His capacity for making non-instinctive, creative, decisions is an indicator of his difference and his humanity.

Chapter Six

CONVENTIONS AND GOOD MANNERS

IT IS possible to think of a very simple way of life in which we are isolated and as nearly as possible, self sufficient, but such an existence is bound to be extremely primitive. It will lack hospitals, schools, transport, all the activities and amenities which depend upon human co-operation and, even so, the sexual urge will demand a relationship with another human being.

Despite our individuality and the awareness of self which seems to be our very nature, we are dependent upon each other and the separateness which occurred, if you like, when the umbilical cord was cut, is illusory.

To understand this consider a road with two vehicles travelling towards each other, each driven by a man. In this simple and common situation the life of both is at hazard and depends upon both conforming to a standard of behaviour. Look down upon a busy main route and you see an exceedingly complex situation of human relationships in which a single failure to conform to agreed codes can bring about disaster for many. It is easy to see that in any society there have to be accepted ways of doing things which make possible commerce, manufacture, transport, education and all the facilities which we need. It is also easy to see that the same sort of thing applies in a bee hive or an ant hill and that blind acceptance of conventions is not enough.

But having seen that there is a warning in the ant hill we must still agree that behaviour patterns are necessary. To some extent they can be enforced. But most of them do not have to be enforced because people understand the necessity. They accept the fact that they have to live with other people and in their actions they accept a responsibility to conform. A man who ignores the rules of the road is rightly called *irresponsible*. Civilized life depends upon such acceptance of responsibility as is implied in observing the rules of the road. There are two sanctions against the man who does not behave responsibly. One is danger to himself. It is in his own interest to conform and he may die if he does not. The other is the law which exists to protect those who do act responsibly against the danger from those who do not.

Here we begin to see a very simple morality which must exist in any community irrespective of any external code or religion and whether there is any such thing as God or not. At first sight it may look as though this morality consisted in obeying the agreed code of behaviour within the society, but this is to look at the surface of the matter and not at its inner meaning. The laws or conventions of the society are not to be observed because they themselves are morally right but because to ignore them within that society would be irresponsible and neglect to conform would cause trouble, damage, confusion, possibly death. The obligation of living in any community is to observe the pattern which is necessary to it as a social organism because one accepts the principle of responsibility to the other people in the community. Only then can civilized communities exist.

It is often said that all morality is just a matter of convention or opinion because what is wrong in one place is right in another. Thus it is argued that because a man can have four wives in Arabia there is nothing morally wrong with bigamy in England where it is illegal. This is as silly as arguing that there is nothing wrong with driving on the left hand side of the road in France because just across the channel in England people do drive on the left. The moral obligation is to behave in a responsible way by driving on the left in England and on the right in France and by not having more than one wife at a time in America despite what they do in Arabia. It is totally irresponsible and dangerous to drive on the wrong side of the road. It is open to anyone to advocate a change in the rule of the road and there is no moral law about one side or the other being right by nature but until the convention has been changed by agreement it is irresponsible, and therefore in a very practical sense wrong, to drive on the *wrong* side.

In thinking about what is right and wrong we must consider the consequences of action in the situation in which action is contemplated. Over a wide range of human activities, such as driving on roads, paying bills, eating in restaurants and going to lavatories, the simple morality of observing social conventions, which it would be irresponsible not to observe, makes life easier for everybody and need cause no trouble to anybody. The underlying principle of it is that we can only enjoy the advantages of civilized life if we do accept the responsibility of conforming to necessary conventions. The conventions themselves may be questioned and judged by standards which we will discuss presently, but in general we may say that they are like oil in a machine which would otherwise seize-up. Observing the social code makes life easier and releases energies for creative endeavours.

But we must insist that we observe the conventions because we are responsible people, not because they are in themselves right or wrong. This becomes very clear when we move into another social environment. Having learned to drive on the left we now find it necessary to drive on the right. At first sight the old adage, 'When in Rome do as the Romans do' looks like good common sense but like most 'common sense' answers to important questions it is inadequate. If you come from a country where only one wife is allowed to a country where two are legal, and you marry a second wife there, you will be in trouble if you take her back home. Your first wife will judge the affair by the standards of your own community, Your second wife will have to fit into an alien situation where she is regarded as an illegal import. You may try to convert your own community to polygamy but this is likely to be a long term operation and meanwhile your first wife, your second wife, you, and possibly the children of both, are suffering from the consequences of what you have done. Clearly great difficulties can arise by doing in Rome as the Romans do. Clearly the accepted conventions of our own society can create moral problems and we need to be aware of the great difficulties created by morality itself. No moral code is so good that it is incapable of begetting evil results. Much pain, suffering and sheer evil has been brought about by people who have acted for moral reasons. This is quite well understood nowadays but what is not so often recognized is that many things are only, or mainly, judged to be evil because of the bad effects of a system of morality.

For example, the main objection to an unmarried woman having a child is that an illegitimate child may not get a fair chance in life. It grows up under a stigma which is in fact created by the prejudice and unkindness of 'moral' people who transfer to the innocent child the consequences of their disapproval of unmarried motherhood as being against *their* moral code. Thus many of the evils of illegitimacy are in fact created by so-called morality. By contrast, in the middle ages, in the Norman England of those ancestors who are most proudly remembered in aristocratic pedigrees, a 'love-child'—i.e. a bastard—was thought actually to be a better child than one merely born in wedlock because it was conceived in love—not an unreasonable idea. William the Conqueror was himself a bastard and in a society where illegitimacy carried no stigma the modern evils of illegitimacy did not arise. The evil is in fact very largely the result of the morality which creates the disapproval. Most of the suffering of bastards in the last hundred years has been due

to the cruel morality of so-called Christian people more than
to the immorality of the mother, and not at all to any fault
in the child itself. Most of the political 'criminals' have been
created by the political system which denied them freedom
to disagree.

Every society must have conventions and these are, by
definition, agreements: they work by common consent. They
are not enforced and we can contemplate an ideal situation
in which we might live entirely by convention and consent, without any morals or laws because these would be unnecessary. We are a very long way from achieving anything
like this. It would be the completely civilized state.

This needs to be stresssed because conventions and morals
have been thrown into the same melting pot. They are very
different, and if we want to get rid of restrictive morality
and legal enforcement we need more, not fewer, conventions,
that is, *willingly accepted behaviour patterns*. The great
advantage of a convention is that the individual is free to
be unconventional at will. He is not restricted but has to
accept the fact that being unconventional makes difficulties;
so he will, if he is sensible, reject the common pattern of behaviour only if it is in some way worth while to put up with
the inconvenience. Unfortunately, men being what they are,
it may often be thought advantageous to rebel against convention for one's own benefit and to the serious disadvantage
of other people. An extreme case would be for a man to
murder somebody who annoyed him. Clearly some other
sanction has to apply in our complex and, in some ways, de-
graded society. In relatively primitive small communities
the conventions are seldom transgressed and this gives some
justification for the legends of a golden age when people
were innocent of evil. (Most primitive societies are, and have
had, strong conventions, as is shown in both art and language. Informality, idiom, idiosyncrasy and originality are
modern.)

The popular image of an anarchist is a man who wants to

destroy but in fact he is an idealist. The word anarchy means *without rule* and the true anarchist is one who aspires to a state of being in which everyone behaves well without any laws or government. Such an ideal is probably unattainable in big communities though small groups, like the *kibbutzim*, have come near to it. It is an ideal worth keeping in mind. It underlines the fact, which is unpalatable to many people, that we need *fewer* morals and *fewer* laws and *less*, not more, government. The principle aim of good government should be to eliminate the need for government or, at least, to reduce it. *The essence of government is to facilitate not to control.*

Conventions may relate to relatively minor matters like, how to refuse an invitation, what to wear for an occasion, when to arrive at a party. The absence of conventions makes it more difficult for all concerned: the observance of conventions causes no hardship and may avoid the waste of energy on problems that need not arise. Such energy might be more profitably employed. In our present condition it would be worth while to devote a great deal of effort to evolving new and convenient conventions or, if we prefer to call them something else, agreed and mutually acceptable behaviour patterns. We waste a great deal of time for the lack of these. In ordinary, *conventional* human relationships we should know what to expect. There is then scope for the exceptional to be exceptional. It is a 'frightful bore' or 'awful drag' being exceptional all the time.

Until man becomes really civilized, conventions are not enough. People in general have to be protected against rogues. The problem arises that a so-called rogue may be a genius with something very important to contribute to the progress of mankind. Probably he is not, but the creative exception, the genius, is so important that we must be very careful not to mistake him for a villain, and so deprive ourselves, and the human race, of what he has to contribute.

The herd instinct is hostile to the exception and the reason for this lies deep in our *animal* nature. We have an instinct to breed true, to reject the mutation and yet, in spite of this, civilization has taught us that the mutation, the genius, may be immensely beneficial in changing us. Our basic instinct is to stay the same, like gorillas and trout, but our human difference originated in, and depends for development upon the contribution which the *exceptional* man or woman can make. Difference, uniqueness, the exceptional are the roots of our success as a species, the reason why we are not 'just animals'. So in accepting the value of conventions we must stress that they are not fixed rules but acceptable behaviour patterns which may change with improvement in ourselves. They should help us to live, not inhibit originality.

Observance of conventions is linked with politeness, but politeness has another ingredient which is *consideration for the feelings of other people*. Animals seem to be polite and in so far as man is rude he is below animal standards of behaviour. This cannot be counted to his credit. The idea of *polite society* is valuable and most of the periods in human history which have made significant contributions to the art of living have observed the value of good manners. This is something we have to re-learn if we are to justify our own age in the history of man.

Conventions and good manners are not insincere any more than the oil in an engine. In considering the value of conventions and good manners in our lives let us remember that most people are ordinary and un-original. Conventions and manners make life easier and more pleasant and they have the great advantage over laws that they do not inhibit people who are different, people who have something new and valuable to contribute to human development. It may be odd to flout the conventions but it is not criminal.

Chapter Seven

CONVENTION, COMMUNITY AND LAW

WE ARE over-governed and our society is cluttered with a huge overburden of antiquated institutions, unworkable rules, out of date customs and creaking administration which legislates frantically to cover up its obsolescence. But our hope must lie in civilization, not in the rejection of it, even to sustain our present population, let alone cope with expansion.

If civilization broke down we would go back to a life of violence and misery. Most of the comforts and conveniences we now take for granted have been built up by centuries of effort. They depend for continuance upon goodwill and co-operation, without which such things as railways, hospitals, electric light and power, telephones, industry and even shops, would be impossible.

If there were no laws and no standards of behaviour violent men would try to do as they liked. They would fight each other and a few would survive. The strongest and most cunning would gain power for a time but would have no security. Millions of people would starve. Most of the rest would lose the freedom they now take for granted and be enslaved. This has happened in the past and could happen again.

The good conduct and co-operation which make civilized life possible are maintained in three ways:

(*a*) Willingly by people themselves, by goodwill and good manners.

(*b*) By customs which are commonly accepted.

(*c*) By laws which may be enforced.

In a free society laws and regulations are, as far as possible, intended to make sure that everyone will accept the minimum standard of behaviour which is agreed to be necessary for living the kind of life that most people want to live.

But the trouble is that the law can be affected by what some people think is good for the others. For example, in a democratic society 51% of people can make a law which 49% of people do not agree with. It may be very unjust to some of the 49%. In some cases a few people who have influence (such as elected representatives, trade union officials, civil servants and experts) can cause laws, regulations or bye laws to be made without understanding the harm they may be doing to some other people. Some laws are made in a spirit of enlightenment but many laws and regulations are made to protect innocent citizens against a few people who behave badly. The more thoughtless, unkind or anti-social behaviour there is the more laws and regulations have to be made, and the more laws there are the more there is need to enforce them and so the more police. If the police find themselves unable to enforce laws by persuasion and the co-operation of the public they have to become more ruthless in order to do their job. When laws are irksome to a majority of the people not only the police but the law itself may fall into disrespect. When laws are made which cannot be enforced likewise the law and the police fall into disrespect.[8]

We have to have some laws but the better we behave the fewer laws we shall need and the more freedom we shall have. Anarchists are people who believe in a state of society where no enforced laws are necessary because everyone behaves well. This is an ideal which seems to be unattainable but the principle is valuable in emphasizing that self-discipline and good behaviour lead towards greater freedom. Violence and other selfish behaviour lead towards less freedom, more law enforcement and so, in the end, more oppression. It is a mistake to glamourize the criminal. He is really an enemy of society and the price we all pay because of a very few criminals is much higher than most people realize.

Civilized life with all its advantages is precariously balanced. Put in another way the more bad behaviour there is the more policemen we need to have, and the more violent crime becomes the tougher the policemen have to be. Then if they fail civilized life becomes impossible and everybody suffers.

But what is good behaviour and what is crime? We live in a very confusing age and it is not always easy to see what is good and what is bad. Let us look at this in a practical way.

If we do not have a code of behaviour which we ourselves accept we shall have to depend more and more upon law and policemen. This would mean much less freedom and would cause many inconveniences and hardships. Many of the greatest benefits and advances in civilization have come about where men who had special qualities, ideas or talents, were free to make their ideas known, to do their scientific research, or to make something which had never been made before, such as an invention or a work of art or a philosophy. Laws and regulations intended to stop crime can, and often do, prevent the most creative men and women from making their contribution. Everyone has much to gain from freedom but in order to have it we must behave in a way which will reduce the need for laws and restrictions.

Freedom has had to be fought for in the past. To keep it we must avoid creating the conditions which produce tyranny of any of the kinds which had to be fought against. In some western countries we tend to take freedom for granted but in fact it is being encroached upon in many ways. Most of these encroachments are for reasons which it is easy to justify in each particular case, but the cumulative effect is becoming serious. It is not difficult to see that a swollen and powerful bureaucracy—a civil service—could become a tyranny. This also has happened before, for example, in the Byzantine Empire, which began with two splendidly creative centuries (c. 330—c. 560) and then lapsed into efficiently organized sterility for a thousand years until it was finally extinguished by Turkish conquest in 1453.

Encroachments upon freedom do not all stem from bad conduct but many of them do. For example, the scattering of litter in roadside woodlands has led to the erection of fences to exclude offenders. The known carelessness of visitors provides an excuse for water boards and forestry commissioners to seal off great tracts of country which could be open if 'the public' could be trusted to behave responsibly.

The word responsibility takes us right back to the primitive tribal beginnings of civilization when the many dangers of life made every member of the community acutely aware of the peril of irresponsible behaviour. In peasant communities young children take their places in the work of the homestead and are responsible almost from the day they can walk. They can mind the cow or herd sheep, pull up weeds, gather firewood. But as civilization progresses the pressing immediacy of the need for responsible behaviour recedes. Nowadays many children grow up without real responsibility even into the middle twenties if they go to a university, though in some studies, notably medicine and architecture, responsibility is put upon them.

The essence of a responsible attitude is awareness of and care about the effect of one's actions upon other people and upon oneself. It may often be difficult to know what is right and what is wrong. It is perhaps impossible to lay down absolute standards but awareness of the effects of action or behaviour and care or concern about these effects is a useful basis. It is fundamental to the healthy existence of human communities.

Responsibility in the modern world demands two qualities which are not obviously associated with it. These are *imagination* and *willingness to learn*.

Imagination is the power by which we can visualize the future effects of what we are doing now. It is a basic part of our power to look ahead. In many of the daily problems of life we learn consequences by experience and remember them as a guide to future behaviour ('the burnt child dreads the fire') but to cope with emergencies and unusual experiences we need imagination if we are to act responsibly.

Willingness to learn is more important now than in the past. Primitive peoples acted responsibly within the narrow limits of their knowledge but a sensible and responsible people could die like flies because they did not know the danger of bad sanitation and the fact that flies could spread dysentery from a single turd to a whole tribe.

In our time there are immense opportunities for learning and responsible behaviour may often depend upon knowledge. It is pathetic to feel responsible towards a drowned man and not know the possibilities of artificial respiration. Nobody can know everything but a responsible person today must be aware of the value of knowledge and know at least that when he does not know the facts upon which to act responsibly he should refer, if at all possible, to someone who does. A sense of responsibility implies respect for fact and truth. It is the very opposite of responsible behaviour to act in ignorance in order to appear responsible as some people do when faced with an accident. To 'pass by on the other side' is, however, rather worse, because it is difficult to envisage anyone so stupid that he could not give some sort of help, if it is no more than to telephone the ambulance, which, in fact, may often be the most useful thing to do, or at least ask if it has been done.

The sense of responsibility, of concern for and involvement with people, is a basic need of society which, as we have seen, is less obvious as social organizations become more complex and less directly in contact with the simpler aspects of nature. Irresponsibility is a cause of hardship, sometimes of acute suffering, and all too often an excuse for the imposition of restrictions upon freedom.

For example, the behaviour of a few rowdies at a sea-side resort results in the imposition of stringent police control which does not improve the holiday atmosphere; yet without it there is a real danger that the beach, promenade and cafés may be unusable by other people and the functioning of the resort may be crippled. A little irresponsibility imposes a quite disproportionate load of trouble, inconvenience and restriction. This is a basic fact of life in human communities and always has been.

We should not allow the complexity of modern life to obscure this need for a sense of responsibility. Indeed, as life becomes more complicated, more affected by elaborate organization and mechanisms, the danger of irresponsible behaviour becomes more serious.

It is a paradox of our time that while the significance of the individual may *appear* to be declining, as we become more conscious of living in a world-community of some four thousand millions of interdependent people, the effects of irresponsible behaviour become accentuated and, in fact, *each individual needs to be more responsible than ever before.* A mad bull rampaging in a farmyard was a formidable peril, but the damage he could do was infinitesimal compared with the havoc a clumsy burglar could cause in an electronics laboratory. On a small farm carelessness might lead to the death of a cow or the fox getting among the chickens but in a nuclear power station it could cause widespread disaster comparable with a volcanic eruption.

In most of our ordinary activities responsible behaviour is easy because we follow established patterns which we have been brought up to observe and they are second nature to us, that is to say, they are acquired in the process of growing up and living in our social and physical environment. Such conventions can be a nuisance but on the whole they are better than laws which have to be enforced. It can happen that conventions acquire the force of moral laws and are backed by the civil law. In such cases (Geneva under the rule of Calvin was an example) a narrow, closed society is created and it may generate explosive pressures and abominable cruelties. The ideal is an open society in which conventions are lightly and gladly accepted as a help to living but are not felt to be restrictive. The ideal is unattainable but life is likely to be most enjoyable in a society which achieves the best balance between convention and freedom so that convention enhances freedom. Decision-making is always difficult and the role of convention is to free man from the burden of deciding upon trivial matters, and upon matters of common consent, in order to liberate his powers for creative decision-making along the unexplored fringe of living. Thus we may achieve the maximum of politeness with the maximum of adventure.

It is commonly assumed that conventions are sterile and ephemeral but in fact they are essential to civilized society. They are the oil which makes it work smoothly without in any way retarding its forward movement.

Men are constantly subject to temptations, the gratification of which would severely curtail the liberty of other people. Murder, rape, theft, incest, arson and perjury are crimes which can, to most men at one time or another in their lives, seem so tempting that the sanction of the law must be brought into the balance against them. Many of the ancient dramas were concerned with the awful effects of indulging such desires in societies (such as the court of Mycenae) where the law could not operate against the offenders. In high politics murder is, as we know only too well, still a weapon which is used with dreadful results. At the highest political levels it is difficult to make the law effective but for most people liberty of unmolested life is assured by the existence and acceptance of law. To be effective law must be acceptable and therefore adaptable to changing conditions. This is the great advantage of the English system of law as opposed to a code of law which is inflexible. Law, like everything else, must be capable of change and adaptation to serve new needs.

But if laws must be changeable so also must customs, and much of our present trouble derives from the continuance of old customs in new conditions ('new wine in old bottles'). For example, in former times, if medicine and nursing could save a child's life it would probably be healthy, and there was no sure means of anticipating that it would not, but modern expertise has advanced so far that it is possible to preserve a child for a half-life in which it will survive paralysed, deformed, incontinent and insane as an enormous burden upon its parents or other people, and to forsee that this will be the consequence of medical treatment. Neither our laws nor our morals have yet accepted the challenge of this new situation which is only one among many unsolved social problems.

The great majority of people seldom have to make decisions outside the framework of established conventions and laws. The question of right or wrong is largely decided by accumulated communal experience and custom and most people wisely accept this. To those who are entrusted with government come special problems, of which a characteristic example is the decision to go to war, thereby rejecting the law against killing and encouraging law-abiding citizens to go out and kill for the survival of their country. It is a very odd fact of history that until quite recently the commandment 'thou shalt not kill' was not seen as being transgressed by soldiers in battle. It would be a mistake to see as hypocrisy what was in fact realism, but again our present situation, created by scientific discovery, needs re-thinking because the logical 'escalation' of killing in battle is the thermo-nuclear bomb and biological warfare.

Apart from government, and to some extent within its framework, the main burden of decision-making falls to people who are called *professional*. The term now needs amplification to include such people as trade-union officials, research workers, engineers, planners, economists, industrial management as well as the services, architecture, law, the church, medicine and the other traditional professions. Stripped of all the humbug the real role of the professional man is that he helps in the making of wise decisions and this is what he is trained for. The professions are organized, more or less effectively, to ensure the responsibility of their members. The essence of being a professional man is that he is *responsible* and, as such, well informed.

Generally the professional man works within a code of practice, architectural, medical, legal, etc. His functions are both executive and advisory. The modern, highly technical world is becoming more and more dependent upon such people. They are not necessarily specially good people nor is their way of life very desirable. They are harassed and constantly aware of their own inadequacy but they are necessary. They have the *burden* of responsibility and they are often rather grey men and women on account of it. As society in general becomes less responsible their job gets more difficult and they become more inclined to establish their limited and specialized standards by administrative procedures.

At this point we must begin to be aware of a danger in modern society which is revealed, on the one hand, by the sense of isolation which exists in the professions and on the other by the vicarious achievement of a football crowd which projects itself, in a curious process of fantasy, into the twenty-two players and the curious figure of the referee on the field.

It is often argued that people nowadays have no opportunity for responsibility, that they are just cogs in the machine, but this is not true. Wherever we look at the fabric of modern society, and the environment which we tolerate in industrial areas, there is abundant opportunity and each person could make a choice between being passive or responsible. Under present conditions the vast majority of people prefer to be passive. They prefer to evade difficult decisions, to grumble ineffectively and not to accept challenge. A wry situation is exemplified in the miner's cottage on a worked-out coalfield where the family refuse to move and sit watching the television image of pioneers in waggon trains to the wild west. Man is not exempt from nature's inexorable law *adapt or perish*. The extent to which society should cushion the individual against the operation of this law, bearing in mind the need of society itself to adapt, is one of the problems we need to think about very deeply and effectively. It is not an *easy* problem and this highlights the special characteristic of our age, that nothing is easy.

Scientific and technological progress has eliminated many of the practical challenges which were almost overwhelming to our great-grandfathers but it has substituted for the old difficulties the challenge of adapting to an environment which is substantially different because of our own achievements, and we have very little accumulated experience of this problem. An enormous growth in the desire for education seems to be necessary and it may appear that, whereas in the pioneer society of America in the eighteenth century, courage, honesty and quickness with a gun—the attributes of a wild west hero —were the prime necessities of survival and progress, and in the war-torn Europe of nations, from Napoleon to Hitler, a willingness to die *en masse* for one's country was necessarily admirable, so in the world of the future a quick and educated mind and skilful, delicate fingers are essential equipment for those who wish to rise above the level of neo-serfdom.[9]

It looks as though there must be enforceable laws in any society but the need for these will be diminished, and freedom enhanced, by education and by the development of a sense of responsibility. The contrary is *apathy* which is, perhaps, the greatest modern danger to the survival of mankind. It was originally a Greek word and it means, literally, *not-feeling*. It is almost the opposite of sympathy which means *feeling-with*. Many young people in Western Europe regard it as a compliment to call someone *sympatique* or *simpatico* and it is unfortunate that the word is not used in English in this sense of being in touch with other people, of sharing with them at the emotional level.

The Stoics, a school of philosophers who strongly influenced declining Roman civilization, thought, on the contrary, that apathy was a very desirable attitude because it
was 'the extinction of the passions by the ascendancy of
reason'. Stoicism is the prevailing philosophy of many people
today and especially of technologists and technicians, that
large class of men and women who are trained rather than
educated and who tend to implement technically sensible
programmes without any care for the way they affect people.

Apathy means no feeling of involvement, loss of interest,
dispassion, lack of a sense of concern and, obviously, irresponsibility. It was apathy which allowed a small minority of
Germans to erect the paranoiac Adolf Hitler as a dictator
and in our own time the greatest danger of thermo-nuclear
war would seem to stem from lack of confidence in the value
of preserving peace, loss of concern for the need to guard
against ignorance and irresponsibility at the high levels of
decision making, in other words, from apathy.

If this is so how can we combat apathy? Not by imposing
some system or organization. Zest for life can only come from
a sense of purpose and involvement in something worth while.
We have long passed the stage, if indeed there ever was one,
where any mere reorganization of anything, from Church to
State, is going to provide the answer. It can only grow in the
consciousness of individual men and women, work like a
yeast through people and so change their institutions. Freedom is a prerequisite.

The role of law in any society should be to preserve freedom, to restrict those acts by individuals or groups within a
society which would damage the rights of other people. But
what are their *rights*? To decide what rights to protect and
what intentions to restrict we have to make value-judgments
for the people within a society. These need not be the same
for all people in all societies—indeed in the interests of variety
and freedom on a world scale it is desirable that they should
vary from place to place. But it is not the function of lawyers

to make value-judgments outside the administration of the law itself. Values are not their business, but any society, in establishing the pattern of law and order which is necessary for its proper functioning, must consider the question of values and morality. There is urgent need for reconsidering the nature of morality, but before we can do so here we must look at some of the underlying assumptions and particularly at the problem of *work* to which so much current morality is related. We shall return to morality as such in Chapter Twelve.

Chapter Eight

THE FALLACY OF THE
WORK-STANDARD

IN THE past there was great need for human sweat and toil.
Man saw this work in the ploughing of fields, the building of
walls, the making of roads and bridges as the prime condition of progress. The humblest labourer could believe, if he
chose to think about it, that what he did added to human
achievement. The 'old proud pageant of man' was sustained
by work. Progress and wealth were the product of work and
the major limitation upon wealth was the availability of
labour. There is an inn at Chenonceaux called proudly *Le
Château et Bon Laboureur* (The Castle and Good Work-
man). This sums up the situation as it was.

Superimposed upon the pattern of labour were devices
whereby a small number of people obtained a large share of
wealth out of all proportion to the work they did, but even
so, there was some justification for the belief that those who
discharged high responsibilities in government did a job
which deserved a lavish reward. The by-product of personal
wealth was leisure for those who cared to have it.

Most people had little leisure. There was the weekly rest
day when they were supposed to attend to the needs of the
soul. Taken seriously the Christian sabbath was certainly not
leisure in any ordinary sense. There were festivals which
mostly had a functional as well as a religious basis and the
pattern of behaviour on these occasions was stereotyped:

feasting and charity at Christmas, dancing and mating on May Day.

For the lord in his castle, as for the monk in his retreat, there was a fairly strict routine of conventional activity. One has the impression that nearly everybody was occupied nearly all the time. Even the furniture tells this tale: it was not for lounging and with an appallingly high death rate even bed was a place of activity and labour.

But the healthy cheerful dawn to dusk working habits of an agricultural society suffered a disastrous change when they were exploited by raw industrialism. What do you want to be when you grow up? was a question which a child was seldom asked in the eighteenth century. Until the industrial revolution a boy's career was largely determined by the circumstances of his birth. If father was a king, son was a prince, first, second or third reserve for the monarchy. (In this small occupational group it is still difficult to opt out and choose one's own career.) If father was a ploughman Tom would, in all likelihood, also be a farm hand. The merchant's son would be placed in the counting house to learn the business; the brewer's boy and the tailor's son likewise would follow their fathers' trades. The squire's eldest would succeed him and there was a problem in what to do with the younger boys. The church and the armed services provided the common answers. Among tradesmen apprenticeship gave some opportunity for interchange, but usually it would be fixed up between the fathers. The baker's youngest lad was bound to the smith who only had daughters. Choice of career was rare and where the opportunity to choose existed it was often hazardous and outside the general pattern. By and large people accepted rather than sought their occupations. They were like seeds which may look alike but one will grow into a cabbage, another into a turnip and a third will bear brussels sprouts, and this seemed natural among men.

The nature of the seed is still probably more important than we care to admit but nowadays there is a great variety of opportunity to chose one's job, not only as a boy or girl but later in life if one wants to change.

This new freedom profoundly affects our way of life and in many respects it makes old conventions of thought and behaviour irksome or inadequate because they were evolved for people who had no say in what they were to be.

When it did become possible to choose, the question was still 'What do you want to be?' not 'What do you want to do?' and this is a hangover from the earlier condition. In the old days a man was identified with his job to a far greater extent than he is now. His very name came from his job—Miller, Smith, Fletcher, Fuller, Baker, Brewer, Taylor. Even the aristocracy followed this pattern taking the name of land for their own, signing themselves Huntingdon, Devonshire, Northumberland, as they still do. The lords spiritual did likewise, taking the name of their sees—William Winchester or Henry Lincoln.

To a very large extent a man was his work or his appointment. Without his functional place in the structure of society he was a vagrant, a man of straw. Even the artist had his slot, plying his trade of picture-making, sign-painting and the like. The musician, though often a wanderer, likewise had his place as the names Piper and Fiddler testify.

This is a subject upon which we might dwell and no doubt what has been said is over-simplified, but it is only the background and for the moment it must remain thus, very lightly sketched.

Freedom to choose a job has come about in the development of an economy based upon industry. Yet old attitudes persist and within the new industrial pattern men and groups of men have fought tenaciously for the identity of their jobs and the right to remain in them for life. Hence the demarkation disputes and resistance to redeployment and re-training. Many people do still feel that they have an inalienable right to be sustained in their own trade as miner, riveter, bricklayer, even town councillor, no matter how the needs of the community for such services may change. The old idea that a man is his job in some deeply mystical way dies very hard and slowly. Parallel with this is the even more deeply rooted notion that a woman's status is that of her husband and of his job. It is a harsh, blind, cruel and now, thank goodness, obsolescent attitude to life. The question 'What do you want to BE?' should no longer be answered by the name of a job. But in a world where more and more work is done by fewer people we still think of men and jobs in the old ways.

In the nineteenth century it was commonly thought, and many people still think, that a man justifies himself by work; but along with other old-fashioned ideas that has been eroded and needs to be questioned. It was a hideous idea that if a man could not get a job he was 'useless', and it was not so much a matter of what other people thought: the unemployed man himself had been brought up to believe in work as the reason for living. If he could not 'get a job' he was on the scrap heap.

Modern methods, including automation, are reducing the amount of work there is to be done and at the same time the population is increasing.[10] This is a stark and challenging problem.

The 'upper classes' have never believed in the sanctity of work. For example, eighteenth-century aristocrats, such as the famous Horace Walpole, Earl of Orford and Richard Boyle, Earl of Burlington, seem to have believed in the quality of their lives, not in justifying themselves by work. They were busy and happy men but they did not have to 'work for a living'. That was an idea which was good for the 'lower orders'. The people they called, quite correctly, 'the working class'.

It is a pity that most social thinking since the eighteenth century has been concerned with eliminating privilege and trying to bring the aristocracy down to the working-for-a-living level. It was probably necessary and the only way to social improvement in the nineteenth century but it has not prepared us for an age of rapidly increasing leisure. It is very hard to get rid of the ideology of an age of grinding poverty. Few of us are so well off that we can see the possibilities which are now open to us and because of this many people are actually afraid of leisure. They find it boring. The common view of life needs to be turned upside down if we are to cope with the amount of leisure which is now being forced upon us. We have to see the Industrial Revolution as an interlude and the challenge now is to 'the working class' to live like kings.

Often men act for reasons which they do not understand. For example, in fighting for shorter working hours and higher pay they do not realize that they are caught up in the main stream of social development which will force these things upon them in any case, whether they want them or not. Men are very prone to fight the battles of yesterday and fail to see the real problems of today.

At low levels of social development work is a necessity and men make a virtue of it. A few, the aristocracy, contract out of this and despise the mere workers. They cultivate a higher way of living but under the old conditions it was very much open to criticism and to abuses. (This will still be a problem.)

There have been other kinds of person who have not been justified by work. Among them are the poets, the social reformers and the saints.

Most people in advanced industrial societies now have sufficient leisure to cultivate their lives outside and apart from their work. One may reasonably say that one's 'job' is the necessary tribute or tax that one pays to society. It is required, in return for one's wages, that there should be a contribution of labour for making what is needed or providing services, such as teaching or nursing, which the community wants. But this is not the justification of one's life. It should take a place in life and a job should be done as well as possible, partly because it is an obligation which is owed to society, but also because the quality of one's work reflects upon oneself. But if society does not require a man's services he is not finished—on the scrap heap.

Long ago we accepted the idea of 'public assistance' and 'the dole'. These were nasty misunderstanding names which in fact recognized the necessity for society to provide for those it could not employ. It was really a recognition of the fact that man is not justified by work—and that was the real reason why so many people hated the dole, both those who received it and those who, in a sense, paid it.

But if we abandon work as the justification for living we have to think of another basis for our lives and this is difficult. Work is in fact an easy way out, a soft option. Take it away and man is face to face with himself and the *real* problems of living.

Does any man who loves a woman measure his love by her efficiency as a wife and mother? Does any woman love her man simply because he is a good worker?

Work is something which has to be done. It may be done by all or only some members of a community. There used to be so much of it, and the profits from labour were so small that most people had to work very hard. Now machinery takes the place of a great deal of human labour and men and women are forced back upon the kind of qualities which endear them to each other, their qualities as people, not as workers.

It is an odd fact that this problem of adjustment is most acute in the upper middle classes, among administrators, professors, scientists, civil servants, business management, and all those, in brief, to whom the phrase 'rat race' applies, that section of society which is, subconsciously, most tenacious of nineteenth-century standards having achieved its position largely by success at school and hard work—'the meritocracy.'[11] For them there is surprisingly little leisure. They solve the problem by the luxury of working too hard. Much of the work is self-generated (Parkinson's Law).

For the so called working classes the problem of leisure is becoming increasingly acute. The sense of fulfilment in work is diminishing. For a great many people work is boring and repetitive. There is little sense of a job well done and there is the looming fear that an electronic machine will make them redundant.

In fact, if a man or woman is doing a job which a mere robot could do as well, he or she ought not to be doing it.

But there is another kind of work. Work for a living is usually quite different from work we do for its own sake, because it wants doing and we want to do it. Examples of this sort of work are, youth club leadership, honorary secretary-ships, committee work, missions, voluntary service overseas, or, for that matter, playing tennis which requires strenuous effort and cultivated skill, usually employed to no end beyond playing the game.

If we could learn to live the way we play games the problem would be more than half solved. But the outstanding fact to be noted here is that if we want to play a game well we have to be prepared to learn. Neither football nor chess are easy to play. The challenge of leisure is a challenge *against* laziness.

This brings us back to the earlier idea of what sort of people we want to become. The attitude we have to the work we do is part of our whole way of living. If we regard our work as a contribution to the well-being of the community we owe it to them, and *to our conception of ourselves*, to do it well. But it is not the purpose of life.

It is worth recalling that we have no record of Jesus doing 'an honest day's work' in his life. He was certainly a very great man but his greatness was in the quality of his being: what he did came out of that. The same may be true of other great men, some of whom worked hard but their greatness lay, not in their work, but in, perhaps, a single idea.

We hear a great deal these days about *work evaluation* and a proper *rate for the job*. In fact it is only possible in a very narrow sense to evaluate any work, even at the artisan level. In administration, teaching, medicine, design and a great number of other activities the quality of the work done is almost impossible to evaluate and, above the minimum level of efficiency required to retain the job at all—and this can be very low indeed—the standards are set by the worker himself. Take, for example, the case of a doctor in a busy hospital. By normal standards his hours of work are outrageous and he would have good reason to be resentful. In fact he probably does a good job, but *how* good a job is something he has to work out for himself and part of the problem will be resisting the temptation to flog himself to the point where he becomes inefficient. He might even have to endure the criticism of being lazy while people are dying in order to keep himself fit enough to achieve his own high standards of performance. This can apply particularly to a surgeon as it can to an artist or a teacher. And at the industrial level quality and efficiency of work are very hard to recognize. Trade union organization is generally against such recognition and protects the average worker against the possibility of exploitation as a result of superior work by another worker. Health, stamina, punctuality, emotional stability, power of concentration, aptitude for learning, quickness of eye or hand, all these things relate to the quality of work and its value, but in our necessary regulation of life by work, in the post-industrial revolution phase of civilization, we have, to a very large extent, taken the pleasure out of work in order to make it the basis for a measure of social equality. Now we are faced with the collapse of the work-structure, with the disappearance of the need for much of the work that used to be required, and we shall have to think afresh about the place of work in our lives.

The trouble is that our economy has been based upon work but it is changing to an economy based partly upon work but increasingly upon equipment. The assumption that money represents goods and services is no longer adequate.

The provision of goods—that is the things we need to buy—depends increasingly upon the possession of raw materials and automated processing equipment.[12] A labour component remains but, as for example in the steel industry, more and more steel can be produced by fewer and fewer people provided that the capital equipment is available. If we continue in our present and ingrained ways of thinking about work and wealth it is foreseeable that, with the decreasing need for labour and the increase of population, people will become a liability and the age of the common man may lead to the age of too common man. Just as in business the management has to 'streamline' its labour force and find ways of operating more efficiently with fewer workers so the larger organization of the state may have to recognize the 'redundancy' of a considerable proportion of its population. This suggests the science-fiction nightmare of a retraction of the human race from many millions to a few super-men, or even a single brain, controlling a world-wide automation. Science-fiction writers have fulfilled one of the essential roles of the artist in society by exploring this possible consummation for the human race—the take-over by the tools.[13]

The fact is that *man is not justified by work*. The idea that he is belongs to the nightmare of the nineteenth century. In other ages only slaves have been justified by work.

It is arguable that there is a natural division among men and that the role of some is like that of the worker bees in a hive while the higher achievements of the human species, art, science, religion and philosophy, perhaps even love, are necessarily reserved for a minority. Some men, Aristotle argued, are natural slaves. It is mainly to Christianity that we owe the belief that men are equal in some absolute sense which is expressed by saying that they are equal in the sight of God. It is a very valuable belief indeed and one which we should discard at great peril. Upon it rest most of our ideas of justice, compassion, social welfare and the 'rights of man', the entitlement to life, liberty and equality before the law. In fact we may trace back, beyond Christianity to Aristotle, the roots of the nineteenth-century belief in the sanctity of work. Slavery was necessary to civilized societies in the ancient world and Aristotle accepted this as fact. Our recent ancestors, trying to cope with the immense opportunities of emergent industrialism but conditioned by the teaching of Jesus, substituted for slavery the moral necessity for work. Industrial prosperity had to be founded upon belief in work. Now the necessity for so much work is receding. We can no longer allow it to be the basis of our social economy because it no longer is the basis.

We have the opportunity to move forward into an era when the quality of living which was hitherto only possible for a few people in palaces, monasteries, universities and other privileged situations, will be open to a great many more. Just how many is an interesting question which is probably impossible to answer at present. *It depends upon what people want.*

Chapter Nine

ACTIVITY OR WORK

WE HAVE become used to the idea of 'working for a living' and we need to remind ourselves that even in the past it has not always been necessary and in the future it may not be generally possible. In many primitive societies, especially in warm damp countries, there is a natural limit to the amount of work it is reasonable or possible to do and people develop the arts of leisure. In more civilized societies there have always been other ways of 'getting a living'. Among these are trade, which may involve very little of what most people would call work, but a great deal of risk, and trade has rightly been regarded as a valuable human activity which, incidentally, provides work for other people who lack capital, acumen, or the flair for taking successful risks. There is income from the ownership of land. This may be 'un-earned' but in many cases it has been increased by good management which again does not involve regular hours of toil for a wage but is socially beneficial. Priests and monks, as well as university scholars, have been maintained out of endowments and offerings. Their contribution has been valuable to society, and recognized as such, but not work in the ordinary sense. It is a symptom of our morbid preoccupation with work that universities are changing from places where people could think to places were people work and this is a very great loss. Some men have lived by gambling and it is a pathetic symptom of the moral bankruptcy of British egalitarian work-centred society that gambling flourishes exceedingly among us. The man who wins 'the pools' is envied by the millions who hope they might do so one day. The question of 'deserving' does not seem to arise; it is 'good luck' not 'unfairness' and the growth of gambling (which has an interesting parallel in the declining years of the Roman Empire) is perhaps a natural protest against the work-centred society.

Industrialization and science, together with the natural build-up through time of resources such as roads, bridges, airports, parks, factories, housing and other *assets*, have increased prosperity and we have undergone a beneficial social revolution which has gone some way towards an even share-out of wealth. The completely egalitarian society was, and for some people still is an ideal, but it is an interesting question whether anybody really wants it with sufficient conviction to be willing to lower their own standard of living in order to raise the standard in a poorer country—if this is indeed possible.[14]

The truth is that many people in the past, and not a few in the present, did not and do not, in the ordinary sense, work for a living and though social puritans are eager to see signs of decadence and evil in such people there is no very substantial evidence for believing that work makes people good and people who live without working for a living go bad. In short, work is *not* a pillar of morality nor is it the best basis for a good life. What matters is not that a man should have to work for a living but that he himself should wish to be active. We could cite innumerable examples of men, now and in the past, who have worked hard without receiving any payment and it used to be considered an almost essential qualification for many important jobs that one had a private income, that one did not have to do the job for the sake of the money. There are, indeed, grave disadvantages in having men in responsible, decision-making positions who cannot afford to resign over a question of conscience or principle.

We do not have to choose between our present condition

and a return to eighteenth-century privilege. We must move forward, not back into systems which have been naturally and beneficially superceded. The key to the problem is our attitude to work, and our persistence in linking work with income is an anachronism.[15]

A remarkable symptom of the malignancy of our work-centredness is to be seen in our dreary, shabby and blighted industrial areas. In many of these there is a good deal of what we call 'under-employment' as well as unemployment, yet all around there are jobs that want doing. The local Council may even be aware of what wants doing but it *can't afford* to pay men and women to clear up the mess, to plant trees, make parks and boating pools, clinics and nursery schools. It might seem obvious that people who have nothing to do should set about the work by voluntary organization and so make their town a much better place to live in and, probably, improve its prosperity as a result of this. But in our crazy work-for-a-living society they would be in bad trouble because they would be doing for nothing what might be done for pay (even though it won't) and so 'depriving' men of work. Given the present economic system of payment for work it is difficult not to sympathize with those who prohibit voluntary work; but the economic system is crazy and does not fit the real needs of our society.

What is the alternative? It is not simply a question of altering the pay structure. It is necessary to find a new attitude to living in which ordinary people can regain the pleasure of creative activity, of doing a job as well as possible, and can unleash their *generosity*. We must recognize that the social reforms of the last hundred years, though they were necessary and good in their time, have created new problems and come up against new economic conditions. Once again we must emphasize that change is the inevitable law of life. We have become the meanest people in all history and cost dominates our thinking about almost everything.[16]

The mechanism of change will require a great deal of

thought and experiment but the objective should be clear. It must be *to dissociate wages from work* and if this seems outrageous we should pause to consider what a very long way we have already gone, unwittingly, towards this goal with sickness and unemployment pay, redundancy pay, pensions, etc. We have only a little further to go in order to establish *a basic income irrespective of work*. This would have to be related to overall resources, probably on a regional accounting basis rather than nationally. It would then be possible to re-establish a free market in labour. The gain in happiness would be great and with a new attitude to work would come a new freedom to develop one's own personality and to contribute effectively, if one so wished, to the benefit of the community.[17]

It is probable that under present conditions of increasing automation and expanding population the free-market price of labour would fall. This might encourage the development of special skills and flexibility which would add zest to life and it would make possible the development of many services, personal and public, which we lack.

At present there is a natural tendency to do the job that brings in most money and there seems no very good reason why people should not continue to sell their labour at the highest price if they wish to do so; but given a basic wage, unrelated to work, many people would be wise enough to choose work which they felt to be 'worth while' or specially satisfying to them. After all, if people were not like this in character there would be no staff in our hospitals, no clergy, no social workers and very few teachers. The great majority of people prefer satisfaction in their work to a high income.

It is often argued that if people don't have to work for a living they become socially irresponsible. Some people, it is true, would do nothing, but in the economy of the future this does not matter and the argument is really a nonsense. Many of the busiest people in the world don't work for money. A great deal of work is done free, for charity, and the vast majority of women—half the population—see no direct financial reward for the work they do. I think we may have sufficient realistic faith in the men to believe that the majority wish to lead active and satisfying lives: if not, the women had better take over. We have reached a stage of development at which we can, as a species, at last afford a moderate standard of comfort for each individual in the more advanced countries. This should be the basis for a new social revolution in which the *quality* of living may be developed.

It is no longer sensible to relate wages to productivity in particular industries. It *is* necessary to relate *income* to the resources of the community in which people live. It is possible to replace the old hard idea of work by the idea of free and generous activity.

Chapter Ten

LEISURE AND JOB

WHAT DO men do with their leisure? Mostly they spend it upon some other kind of work which they do for pleasure. Often this work is in contrast to the job by which they earn their living and they bring to it quite different standards. Instead of being concerned, for example with productivity in his factory, the works-manager comes home to his garden and plants out seedlings with loving care, and regardless of the cost of time. Many skilled tradesmen actually ply their own trade, such as carpentry or painting houses, free lance (moonlighting) and enjoy working to their own standards instead of doing skimped work for a contractor. Some people play games which may be strenuous far beyond what any employer dare demand for pay and there is intense satisfaction in playing a game for its own sake, for the quality of the experience whether it is won or lost. Some people sail open boats across the oceans or study nature or archaeology in outlandish places. Some people read, study, develop their minds and enjoy contemplation. Others dedicate themselves to social services and some enjoy administration, trusteeship or committees.

There are a lot of unpleasant things to be said about human nature but it must be admitted that on the whole we are an active species. We like doing things and making things, if only the system will let us, but at present we are caught in a trap which stultifies life for a great many people. This is largely the result of over-correcting old evils by means of institutions which were highly beneficial but have become their opposite by failing to adapt to the conditions they have created.

There is really only one answer to the so-called problem of increased leisure and that is activity. If we do nothing we get bored and irritable. We need freedom to enjoy leisure and we need a vast increase in facilities—everything from playing fields to libraries and retreats for contemplation— but our system has become so constipated that we can't have them. We can't *afford* them although the main part of their cost is labour. We have an enormous surplus of personal energy and skill which we are inhibited from using. It would be great fun for a group of people to build their own neighbourhood centre in spare time but it is practically impossible, and in many people's view socially wrong, for them to do so. We could have a marvellous environment and enjoy ourselves in the making of it if only we could get out of the straitjacket of an out-of-date system.

The answer to the problem of leisure is the release of constraints upon free activity; that is, work undertaken in the attitude of play. We all learn to do this at school but as soon as we grow up our abominable social system clamps down upon the pleasures of activity. This is particularly true in trades where an apprenticeship has to be served and a youth is 'de-educated' into dullness. With luck a man may enjoy the use of his skills at home, in carpentry, painting, gardening, but not in the social context. If, on the other hand, the activity is a recognized sport he may join a team, run a club and even charge for admission.

The increase of automation and the production of most of our common necessities, from motor vehicles to toilet paper, by large industrial plants, is having the effect of standardizing the products so that differentiation is rarely achievable. We are losing the interesting variety of artefacts, and from one country to another the machine-made product is standardized. Even architecture, made from standard factory-produced components, looks much the same from Tokyo to New York whichever way you go. Yet there is satisfaction, not only in seeing hand-made things which are unique, but also in making them; and the increase in leisure which is inevitable seems to offer the opportunity, and indeed the necessity, to re-develop hand skills.

Just as, on the economic level, we should assure a basic personal income as a citizen's birth-right, so on the production level the factories can provide all our basic needs as standard products; but just as the basic wage can free the market in labour, so the increase in leisure can be used to make things again for the joy of making and the beauty of what is made. This could improve the quality of living, both by the making and by what is made to be enjoyed. So the paradoxical result of automated mass production could be, if we wish, the revival of arts and crafts.

This is not idealistic moonshine. It is already clear that in an industrial society with high labour costs, even such necessities as house repairs are difficult to obtain because they depend upon individual skill. But we cannot live by mass production alone if we are to have any quality in our lives, and if we break the work-wages deadlock there is no reason why people should not do 'one-off' jobs and enjoy doing them. There is the argument that nobody likes cleaning drains, but this is not true—some people do enjoy cleaning drains because it is a necessary job with a challenge in it and they have the skill to do it.

It appears, then, that leisure and work are related and overlap. Leisure may be profitable, in that labour or skill may be charged for but in a free market, and artefacts may be sold. It might then appear that a man's main 'work' was his leisure activity and it might be very remunerative. Excellent! This is the way successful artists live and it is one key to the art of living.

But what about a man's JOB?

The first thing to realize is that many people won't have jobs. We have to adjust from saying a man has the misfortune to be out of work to giving him special respect because he has a job to do. Jobs should go to those who are capable of doing them best and we might expect a change of social attitude to develop. If we could achieve a state of mind in which status was related to responsibility undertaken we should be a long way nearer to being civilized and security would no longer depend upon '*holding down* a job'.

It is not the purpose nor the possibility of this book to examine ways and means but only to state some objectives. These cannot be permanent solutions, because change will beget more change and all the challenges cannot, and should not, be anticipated now. Put very simply the aim is that we should accept the logical development of welfare state legislation in Britain[18] and elsewhere and pay a basic allowance to every man, woman and child in their own right. The second stage of earnings would be on the free market. The administrative problem would seem to be to calculate the permissible personal allowance and this probably ought to be on a regional accounting basis. National governments, which came into being during the 'warring states' period of our progress towards western civilization, are not satisfactory except for national war efforts. We should get rid of them. (It is a pity the developing countries have followed our mistaken policies of nationalism.) Regionalism coupled with a two-stage system of incomes, consisting of a personal allowance plus an earned component, would go a long way towards re-establishing the sense of purpose and responsibility which has been lost in industrialized communities.

The tragedy of the present century is that, having been liberated in large measure from toil, by machinery, man has become enslaved to the concept of labour in its own right. We must get rid of this and substitute pleasurable activity. We may also liberate the creative powers of men and women, as we have liberated the creative powers of children in the best of our schools, and if this can be done the character of our lives may be transformed. The glories of the Renaissance would fade into insignificance by comparison with what could be achieved in our time.

Chapter Eleven

ART AND PLAY

MANKIND LOOKS back to a legendary past when, in a state of innocence, he was unencumbered with possessions and responsibilities. The Garden of Eden, and other paradises imagined by man, are somewhat idealized but they reflect the reality that animals and primitive peoples, under reasonably favourable conditions, do have time and the inclination to play. Song, dance and story telling, decorating oneself and one's home with bright designs, sitting in the shade of an olive tree and making music on a reed pipe with one eye on the sheep safely grazing, these things we have sacrificed in the long working struggle which mythology represents,[19] with sure intuition, as having begun with the appetite for knowledge. (*Genesis 1*).

Ever since man set about the colossal task of harnessing nature to serve him he has paid the price in sweat and toil until, in the industrial cities of our own time much of what makes life sweet has been lost. They have become ugly, noisy, stinking prisons in which people feel more and more frustrated and irrelevant. This is partly because of bad design and carelessness but the remedy does not lie in better planning for the town planners and architects are, on the whole, making things worse because they have no vision of a better way of life. With an increasing population our environment will get worse, not better, until we achieve a new sense of values. The key to a new world is a change in our attitude to work.

In the long tunnel of progress, for a hundred or more

71

generations, successful communities have risen and lived by
work, productive work which has been the basis of wealth.
Primitive communities which did not join in the struggle,
and remained in tribal simplicity, were open to exploitation
or were left far behind. Now that some of them are demanding the fruits of the struggle for progress to which they have
not contributed, it seems, perhaps not unnaturally to the
developed nations, somewhat unfair that they should claim
what they have not worked for. This is a measure of the
distortion which work-worship has wrought in us. Generation
after generation has worked to live and morality and education have been geared to the need for work. The achievement
has been enormous *and worth while* because we have come
to the end of the tunnel. But to get out into the fresh air
on the other side of the mountain of toil we have to change in
ourselves: we might almost say 'be re-born of the spirit'.

As things are the primitive communities are demanding
work, blindly accepting the values of the world from which
the advanced societies have the opportunity to emerge and
take the primitive peoples with them. It is no accident that
great artists have recently learned afresh about art from
primitive societies and turned away from the toilsome manufacture of art-treasure to spontaneous enjoyment of artistic
activity. The artists who, throughout history, have led man
more than he realizes, are already re-capturing the value of
play. Picasso is a prophet. It is one of the great ironic jokes
of all time that his toys are solemnly collected by sad-faced
tycoons and dumbly beheld by gallery-crawling crowds who
take in so-called culture like medicine.

Work is scarce and getting scarcer. If we stay in the tunnel
we shall fight for work and the right to work and the right
to be rich according to our work, and in the process we shall
destroy ourselves with horrible weapons we have *worked* to
perfect. And yet there are immense opportunities for work
which could be released if only we stopped worshipping
work and making it the core of our social organization. There

are infinite opportunities in our spoiled environment for doing things and making things and having 'joy in the making'[20] but they are outside the tunnel. To get outside we must accept the idea that members of a community are entitled to a living irrespective of whether they work or not. This is not idealistic: it is a practical necessity. In Britain we have almost reached this state in practice but without acknowledging its value. To go off the work-standard seems to many people a step into moral chaos.

Work is not the proper basis of morality but it became necessary to make it so while we were in the tunnel of material progress based upon labour. Morality is the subject of the next chapter but here and now let us consider play as an alternative to work.

The present state of association football as a sport is an indicator of the degree of corruption which can take place in play by applying the work-standard to it. Most lovers of the game deplore its degradation and want to see it played for its own sake. That is the way it should be. We can turn play into work by doing it for a purpose other than playing the game. We may, for example, play football for national prestige and go out to win at almost any cost. It then becomes work. We have seen the work-standard applied to the Olympic Games with sad results and they have lost almost entirely their significance, as invented by the ancient Greeks. We can even turn play into work by undertaking the activity of the game in order simply to keep fit but without enjoyment. The essence of play is that it contains its own fulfilment. The joy is in the doing and the *doing well*. If there is a functional reason for play it is part of the experience of living which is the subject of the final chapter.

It is difficult, perhaps impossible, to define the point at which play becomes art but on the other hand it is possible to recognize, in the play of children, a preparation for life in its primitive forms. Cowboys-and-Indians, French-and-English and other variations of opposition between two sides, reveal a primitive function of play which was to prepare the child for the hard realities of life. Likewise the girl who plays with dolls is preparing, in play, for the task of motherhood. Children's play is often serious and a preparation for work but the play of adults is mature play, undertaken for its own value.

There are two main branches of play, art and sport. Popular opinion is quite right in recognizing that high achievement in both these fields is admirable but both need to be freed from the work syndrome. In sport, admiration should be for the way the game is played and not for the result of the match. In art it is already accepted that the artist makes his achievement within the limits of what he attempts to do. The picture, sculpture, song, sonata or whatever it is, does not achieve validity and quality by direct comparison with other pictures, sculptures, sonatas and songs but by its quality, in much the same way as people do. A work of art is like a person—unique.

Both art and sport are bedevilled by mercenary standards and we need to recover the old innocence of belief in the intrinsic value of sport and works of art. Intrinsic means that the value is not to be assessed by comparison but is inherent in the quality of what is done, whether it is a game of football or a painting.[21]

To many people the idea of incomparable value is repulsive because they are conditioned by the old attitudes to wealth and work but let us consider the beauty of the moon floating through clouds on a summer evening. This is comparable with nothing, judgable by no standards, given to us whether we like it or not, a cosmic happening which will never occur again in quite the same way. It is totally unrelated to ourselves except by the fact of our seeing it and it is, for us, an experience of beauty and mystery.

Man exists on a tiny planet in a vast universe. Work is concerned with the problem of survival but the essence of living is to be open to experience.

Art and play have much in common but, in general, play involves the exercise of faculties for the pleasure of using them well, whether it be in football or in chess. The vocabulary of art and play are substantially interchangeable, as when we rightly speak of a *beautiful* stroke at cricket or *exciting* brushwork in a painting. But though art is related to and rooted in play, and in the exercise of skill, it is not the same. It has wider scope and powers to express emotion, to interpret experience and to explore the unknown by means of the imagination. Art may be very serious, as it is in tragedies such as Euripedes' *Medea* or Shakespeare's *Macbeth*, but its seriousness is not a measure of its artistic merit. Art involves the creation of something which has unity, which is recognizably itself and complete in itself. It is not necessarily any more permanent than a game of tennis.

If we could abandon the work standard most activities could be undertaken in the spirit of play, or art, or both and enjoyed. The need to recover the enjoyment of activity by freeing it from the label of work is very great in our time if we are to recover happiness which, to quite a large extent, we have lost and are in danger of losing completely. Moreover, the opposition of work and play in our present way of life makes work serious and play frivolous, yet in fact when we play a game 'seriously' we take it more seriously than work in that we put the whole of ourselves and every last ounce of effort into the game in a way that very few people are able or even *allowed* to do with their work. Thus the acceptance of a play standard rather than a work standard for our lives involves a greater seriousness and not frivolity. Real pleasure, whether in art or play, in work or love, comes from complete involvement, from dedication and this is the play attitude which we need to recover. Puritan obsession with work and distrust of pleasure has backfired and resulted in an impoverishment of the quality of living. The possibility is that we could live at the intensity of serious art or sport and this would be an enrichment of the quality of living.

Chapter Twelve

MORALITY

WE MAY now return to the questions raised at the end of Chapter Seven and consider the nature of morality and its place in modern life. It is a difficult subject and one which engenders a great deal of anger and prejudice so it will be necessary to look briefly at some historical aspects of morality in order to get it into perspective and see why some of the old attitudes really do belong to the past and not to the present.

Morality may appear to be of two kinds, public and private. The public kind is concerned with agreed standards of behaviour within a community which are necessary for the survival, comfort and well-being of that community. *The Ten Commandments* were the public morality of the Jewish people at the time of their migration from Egypt to Palestine. They comprise:

1. *Thou shalt have no other gods before me.* This demands loyalty to the tribal god and patron with all it implies in loyalty to the community over against all other communities and their patrons.

2. *Thou shalt not make unto thee any graven image— for I the Lord thy God am a jealous God, visiting the iniquity of the fathers upon the children unto the third and fourth generation of them that hate me.* This reinforces the first and gives a stern, clear warning that God's relationship is not only with individuals, but with families and the community, as continuing entities from

generation to generation, which is biologically true.

3. *Thou shalt not take the name of the Lord thy God in vain.* This again insists upon respect for God as the basis of community life.

4. *Remember the sabbath day to keep it holy* is yet again a demand for respect, in that time be set aside for the worship of God, but it also makes the socially wise provision for a day of rest each week.

5. *Honour thy father and thy mother* consecrates the family and gives necessary protection of the old against the vigorous young.

6. *Thou shalt not kill* is a necessary prohibition of murder.

7. *Thou shalt not commit adultery* protects the right of a man to have his own children by his wife.

8. *Thou shalt not steal* protects property.

9. *Thou shalt not bear false witness against thy neighbour* is a protection against scandal and perjury.

10. *Thou shalt not covet*—might seem to verge upon private rather than public morality in that it seeks to control a man's feelings. It is an injunction against envy and jealousy but if we remember the conditions under which it was made, the Jews newly escaped from captivity in Egypt and making their way across the desert to Palestine, probably many of them starving, it may appear as a necessary injunction if the leaders were unable to enforce a sharing of resources, as seems likely. When they arrived in the promised land it took on quite a different significance, favouring the rich against the poor, protecting 'the establishment' and militating against social unrest.

According to the Bible (*Exodus 19* and *20*) the commandments were given by God[22] on Mount Sinai but we may prefer to think that Moses went up the holy mountain in great anxiety about the discipline of the people, released from bondage, faced with the problems of freedom, and subjected to the rigours of the desert trek. No doubt he thought deeply, prayed and believed he had communed with God and worked out the laws under his guidance, so he could honestly come down and present them as the word of God and with the necessary authority. *The Ten Commandments* are a simple and realistic moral code which has so many advantages that it has been used ever since under very different conditions. It does not say some things are right and some things are wrong: it simply says *thou shalt* and *thou shalt not*. It implies that right is obedience to the will of God and wrong is disobedience. There was no problem of anyone not believing in God, *and* other gods. Everybody did.

The Jews believed in a god who was *their* God with a special function of looking after them, if necessary at the expense and to the discomfiture of other people. He was a tribal god. But other peoples, and especially the Greeks, thought of the gods as being capricious and dangerous, differentiated from man by being immortal but certainly not being good to anybody. Thus the Greeks made sacrifices in the hope of winning favours from the gods and they gave a degree of divine authority to their civic organization by identifying it with a patron deity such as Pallas Athene at Athens, but their relationship with divinities was a practical compromise with forces they acknowledged to exist. Questions of morality, of right and wrong, came to be discussed at a philosophical level.

When Christianity became established it drew upon divine authority, as understood by the Jews, but amplified by Jesus who said that God, his father, was the only god and cared for all human beings. This message, this gospel, of a *good* God who cared for all men, rich and poor, and for all races of men, had a very strong appeal as compared with other religions which had much less to offer. But Christianity did not rest only upon the teaching of Jesus; it also incorporated, mainly through St. Paul and St. Luke, a good deal of Greek thought. In the early middle ages it was torn by doubt and dispute about the nature of God: was he the saintly teacher, the man Jesus; or the father figure of the Israelites; or was he the philosophical and mystical concept, the Holy Spirit? This problem was resolved, if not solved, by the device of the Trinity: God was to be conceived as all three in one— God the Father, God the Son and God the Holy Spirit.

So long as the idea of God as a good father could be salvaged the morality of the commandments could be maintained. But in modern times it is this very idea of God as a good father who personally looks after us, each and every one, which has been most difficult to continue to accept. The historical Jesus, as a very good man and visionary teacher is easy to believe in. The idea of a spiritual existence, on a different plane from our own, is difficult to define but not repugnant to reason and has a strong appeal to those men who are attuned to the mystery rather than the physical phenomena of the universe. The essential teaching of Jesus was that men should live together in love, that God is a spirit, that God *is* love. Christian people have, for nineteen centuries, had the enormous advantage of believing in a good God who cared for their welfare and, with the confidence thereby engendered, they have achieved more than any other people in material and social progress. It could be said that by believing in God they have made God as a force to help them and inspire them in adversity. (This raises the interesting question whether, and to what extent, something can exist by being believed.) Certainly having a firm, authoritative moral code, despite its manifest shortcomings, cruelties and injustices, has been a great help in the tunnel of progress. But what happens if we come out of the tunnel?

Unless one believes in a paternal god who decides these things for us it is difficult to assert that anything is absolutely right or wrong, good or evil under all conditions. It is, however, perfectly reasonable to believe in goodness and badness as such but what is good and what is bad in any particular case is a matter of judgment. So far as public morality is concerned the standard of judgment tends to be the consensus of opinion about the aims and values of the community, or the ruling element in the community. Thus, to die for one's country (and by implication to kill for one's country), is good, but to betray one's country is bad. But in fact public morality does rise above pure self-interest. The bad traitor to his own country should be the good friend to the enemy country but he is not so regarded; he is despised because both countries believe in honesty and good faith and regard treachery as evil. Such examples as this have led some philosophers to believe in natural laws of right and wrong but it is not so simple. Consider the case of the traitor to a country which has a very bad government. It may be in the best interest of that country to have its government betrayed to 'the enemy' because that is the only way to get rid of the tyranny and so the traitor may in fact turn out to be a patriot.

Consider also the question of justice, of equality before the law. According to *Exodus 21* (following *The Ten Commandments*) '*if any mischief follow, then thou shalt give life for life, eye for eye, tooth for tooth, hand for hand, foot for foot, burning for burning, wound for wound, stripe for stripe*'. Many people nowadays would consider such a concept of justice as thoroughly evil.

It is necessary for any community to have rules of conduct. They should, however, be regarded as such, not as moral laws. But a moral problem arises when someone breaks the rules. He may have to be punished as a deterrent to himself and others but the question of whether he is good or bad in what he has done rests upon quite other grounds. Jesus, for example, was punished for breaking the rules, not for being wicked. His punishment by crucifixion is one of many examples of men who have, according to subsequent opinion (and it was probably the opinion of Pontius Pilate, his judge) done good by breaking the rules. On the other hand a lout who enjoys bullying old women seems to be bad by any standards. Though excuses may be made for him on psychological or medical grounds, measures have to be taken to protect old women from him.

The function of the law is to guide and to protect, not to judge. At present it tends to be too concerned with judgment and to fail lamentably in protection. The law should not say 'this is right and that is wrong', because it is not competent to do so but it should say 'this is allowed and that is not. If you do that which is against the law you do it at your own peril—but you may be quite right.'

In practice the law of what is allowed and what is not has been formed by generations of experience but most of these generations believed in divine law and retributive justice on biblical authority (such as *Exodus 21*) which is no longer generally acceptable. As we emerge from the tunnel of progress we must look carefully at our accumulated prejudices and ingrained habits of judgment to see what can be discarded and what needs changing. Meanwhile we should not confuse legality with morality.

The common view of morality is that it is concerned with doing right; that moral behaviour is good and immoral behaviour is bad. Every organization, whether it is a small club or a large nation, tends to think its rules or laws are good and the breaking of them is bad, so morality is used to support the law in a way which is not legitimate because it assumes that the law-makers know what is good and what is evil. The attitude of the individual to the law is a moral question *for him* but conformity to the rules of any organization cannot be regarded as necessarily good and moral, nor can non-conformity be necessarily immoral and bad.

Morality is essentially a private matter. It is concerned with the way we live our lives, with our conduct and with our personal relationships, with our aspirations and what we do with ourselves. It would be improper to say how anyone should or should not live their lives, just as it would be improper to say how an artist should paint a picture or a poet write a poem. Living is an art. This means that we need to pay a good deal of attention to the making of our lives because works of art do not just happen. It is not an art which we practise in isolation but, almost inevitably, in consort with other people. It is an art of relationships as well as of activity and contemplation. As with all arts there is much to be learned about it from the achievement and experience of others. Living is the kind of art exemplified in playing in an orchestra: there is scope for soloists and conductors as part of the orchestra. It is valuable to study moral systems but they should be recognized as being systems not codes. By system I mean an organized way of thinking about moral problems; by code I mean a set of rules which one is constrained to obey. It may well be that an individual will find a system of morals, such as those propounded by some religions, is a valuable scaffolding to the art of living but he should accept it voluntarily and recognize that other people may find a different system more valuable.

It is exceedingly hard for human beings, especially for 'good' human beings, to adopt a system of living without wanting to impose it upon others in their own interests. We suffer enormously from people who overflow in moral domination of other people. It is a kind of *aggressiveness* which is one of the primal causes of war (wars of religion, faith and political creed which have been some of the nastiest in all history). Nobody is in a position to know, or to judge fairly, the inner workings of another personality and we are each entitled to respect for our own way of fashioning and living our lives. Society, as we have acknowledged, must make rules of the road in order that we may live in communities, but these are working rules not moral laws.

It is difficult to see how there can be such a thing as 'The Moral Law', or on what foundations it could rest, but this does not absolve us from the necessity to try to do right rather than wrong, even though it is impossible to say specifically what is right and what is wrong. This is not a contradiction. We may have an abstract idea of 'the good' without being able to say what is good in any particular instance, just as we may have an abstract idea of 'money' without having a penny in our pockets. Morality is concerned with our wanting to do right rather than wrong, the good rather than the bad, but it is a personal matter, part of our very existence as human beings, and we shall have to try to see whether there are any ways of discriminating the nature of good and evil which are acceptable in the modern world, apart from the possibility of divine authority, which is remarkably misleading and contradictory if we are to judge by such evidence as is available.

The idea of right and wrong will be the subject of a later chapter but before we leave the question of morality let us consider whether truth, beauty and humour have anything to do with it. If morality is concerned with the way we fashion our own lives it is not purely a matter of good and evil.

'The truth, the whole truth and nothing but the truth' is a legal fiction. It is impossible to know the whole truth about anything, especially about the subjects of evidence in a court of law, but over a wide range of subjects it is possible to say 'this is true and that is false'. It is true that the moon is a more or less spherical satellite of the earth, that it has no atmosphere and is made of rock. It is not true that it is made of cream cheese. Modern science is based upon respect for truth and the great contribution which science has made to human ways of thought is by establishing the nearest possible approximation to 'the truth' as a standard of excellence, indeed as the very basis of the concept of science. It is highly instructive to note that science can only survive and proceed if scientists respect truth and reject what has been proved untrue. If, for example, in a series of experiments, a research worker were to introduce a deliberate false result in order to substantiate a theory of his own, a great deal of completely useless work might be done by other researchers, on the basis of his corrupt results, until at last he was proved wrong. Tampering with the truth does happen in scientific work but it is contrary to the whole concept of science and when it occurs it has the effect of setting back, of retarding rather than advancing knowledge, of making work more difficult not facilitating it.

In contrast with this, political and religious systems commonly discourage the pursuit of truth and men have been martyred for upholding what could be proved to be true. It is arguable, and I think it is true, that these aspects of religion and politics are contrary to the interests of the churches and parties which practise them. It is arguable that telling lies is bad and over a very long period of human experience the truth has tended to prevail. If a thing is untrue it cannot indefinitely be upheld against the truth. It is very hard in many matters to know what is true and what is not. This difficulty is increased by the many people who have a vested interest in falsehood and a fear of truth. There may well be occasions when ruthlessly to tell the truth, or what we believe to be the truth, would be cruel and destructive but in framing our own lives it is useful to accept the fact that nothing which is founded upon falsehood can be very secure, that lies breed lies and that there is a great deal to be said for the basic ethic of science which is, though it is seldom put in quite this way, that the nearest approximation to the truth is good and any tampering with truth is bad.

Beauty is very difficult to discuss. Like truth it is an abstract idea but unlike truth it cannot be tested. There is no way of discovering for certain that one thing is beautiful and another is not. Our experience is that what is beautiful to one person is not pleasing to another. Clearly beauty has something to do with pleasure and our feeling of pleasure. It is thus desirable though undefinable. It is possible to argue that beauty is an ideal towards which everything in our lives should tend. This is worth considering and, because it is a fact of almost universal experience that men do feel for beauty in one way or another, it is worth while considering it as a *value* which we should take into account in our moral attitude to our lives. Some people have said that what is beautiful is good by virtue of its being beautiful. This also is worth thinking about.

Beauty seems to be an innate quality of nature whether we look at the moon and stars or the daisies on the lawn. Flowers, it is true, usually have a function (a few are sterile and appear to be pure exuberance) but many flowers go far beyond what is necessary in being beautiful and horti-culturists can, by breeding, enhance their beauty. This is not interference with nature; it is one part of nature, man, exploit-ing the potentialities of another part of nature because he likes bigger flowers. This propensity of nature to be beautiful is remarkable and our own inability to define, in a philo-sophically satisfactory way, what beauty is, does not stop flowers and sunsets and occasionally human beings from being beautiful. This is a paradox of our own incompleteness. Fortunately our powers of perception and experience are not limited by our intellects.

Humour is part of nature. It is impossible to study the natural world for long without finding this to be true and many animals have a sense of fun—especially dogs. But in man the sense of humour and the faculty of laughter are much more highly developed. The smile is a sexual invitation and commonly regarded as enhancing beauty in a face. Sex, beauty and humour are linked. But humour is much more than this: it is a marvellous kind of oil in the relationships between human beings. It is purgative and destructive of falsity, of pomp and pretentiousness, so it is linked with truth. A sense of humour is closely linked also to a *sense of pro-portion* which is something we shall discuss later. The ability to laugh, especially at oneself—which implies seeing oneself from outside—is an important component of personal morality, that is to say of all morality.

Finally, for those who can accept the system of any religion which implies the existence of a beneficent God the conclusion of this chapter is that morality rests upon the relationship of the individual to God, not to a set of rules. If there are rules they are only part of the religious technique, not the religion itself.

Chapter Thirteen

IS A MODERN RELIGION POSSIBLE?

MOST PEOPLE, whether they are religious or not, tend to associate morality with religion, mainly because Christianity, as a religion, has concerned itself with morality and in many instances has laid down rules of conduct, even to the extent of trying to regulate the behaviour of a married couple in their own bed. It is one of the ironies of religion and morality that the rules have, in some cases, been made by celibates who are not supposed to have had any such experience. It is unfortunate that Christianity, which as a religion has considerable advantages over others, has been confused with morality. As a result of the confusion many people have been alienated from religion and finding the morality propounded by the Church unacceptable they have been incapable of seeing the religion clearly for what it is. A religion is something more than a philosophy, more than a system of understanding the relationship of man, and oneself in particular, to the universe. To be a religion it must predicate the existence of a god in some form. The word *god* is perhaps the most imprecise noun in the whole of our vocabulary. The concept of god can range from a savage idol which demands propitiation by encouraging sadism and all that is most repulsive in man's nature to, 'In the beginning was the Word, and the Word was with God and the Word was God'. (*John 1*.)

The reaction from religion has gone so far with some people

that they may find it difficult to discuss the idea of god at all because they were put off by images of divinity, such as the father figure, the virgin or the gautama. It may help to realize that the word god is no more precise than x in an equation. If we can honestly begin to study the evident phenomenon of religion as though it were an equation, and x might be anything or nothing, we may find the enquiry useful. This applies equally to those who, perhaps rather presumptuously, think they know the nature of God and those who, perhaps equally rashly, assume that God cannot exist. For the purposes of the discussion and in the interests purely of clarity and without any prejudgment, the word God with a capital letter will be used here to distinguish the Christian concept of the supreme divinity.

Most sensible religious people realize that the only sense in which God can be conceived as existing is in a manner and, to an extent which by his nature and ours must be beyond our powers of perception and conception. Men and women have therefore made innumerable approximations and images by means of which to think about divinity and according to the Jewish religion, which is basic in this respect to both Christianity and Islam, the making of a 'graven image' purporting in any way to be a 'representation' of God, is wrong. God was to be kept as a concept and not made into an idol. As a concept in anybody's mind he was inevitably limited to what that particular mind was capable of conceiving. For most people a father or mother figure was about the limit but some people have gone much further.

To go further requires considerable energy and effort and this needs to be stressed. People will devote a great deal of time and energy to improving their putting at golf, deepening their understanding of chess or enlarging their experience of football by travelling long distances to see the game played well: they do not expect to play a musical instrument without study and practice or to grow tomatoes without troublesome preparation of the soil, careful choice of seed and prolonged nurturing of the plants but in matters of religion, as also in the understanding of art, the same people often expect everything to be easy. They think the lesson should be obvious and the benefits should accrue without effort to understand the techniques involved. By mere uncultivated raw intuition they expect the most marvellous works of art to be available to them and they require God, if he exists, to pour himself over them like custard over a pudding with the automatic inevitability of a factory canteen.

It is reasonable to expect a civilized human being to take some trouble to inform himself before dismissing altogether the long-accumulated opinion of mankind that there is some validity in religious experience. It cannot be easy.

The problem of the nature of God is bound up with the problem of the nature of man. In what sense do we exist at all? One answer is 'I think therefore I am'.[23] The physical world used to seem very solid. It was made of rock, water and air out of which grew life in the form of plants and animals. But modern physics has shown that 'solid matter' is made up of particles which are not 'solid' in the old sense at all. They are 'electricity' and matter consists of differences in charge, the kind of difference which exists between the negative and the positive poles of a battery. We perceive the physical reality of the universe because we are instruments attuned to feel certain types of electrical phenomena just as a television set is tuned to receive certain other electrical phenomena and convert them into our kind of currency, the kind of things we can see. So far television is two-dimensional. It is not very difficult to imagine that it might be three-dimensional. What sort of 'reality' would this be? Television comes to us through the atmosphere as waves generated by impulses at the transmitting station. These waves are invisible and could be thought not to exist if there were no television receivers. Is it possible that we ourselves exist in similar fashion, that our 'existence' depends upon receptor-mechanisms? Is it possible that we are in fact an idea—the Word?

What used to be called mysticism is now much nearer to 'reality'.

If we come to this problem from a quite different direction, through the thinking of Taillard de Chardin for example, we may ask in what sense does an idea 'exist'. Is it possible that there is a plane of existence, at one remove from our physical experience, in which ideas, poetry, expressed emotional experience, exist in their own right, a kind of atmosphere of thought which is just as physically real as, for example the ionosphere which we cannot see but which makes radio and television possible instead of allowing the impulses generated at the transmitter to escape into outer space?

The image on our television screen is reflected, as from a mirror, by the ionosphere. Is what Taillard called the *noosphere* (that is the sphere of mind) a possible reality?[24]

The science which deals with these problems is called metaphysics and it has lately been neglected, mainly because acceptable scientific techniques for pursuing studies in this direction have not been worked out. Science is still very largely confined within our own powers of sensory perception. Even scientists still tend to think that what is 'extra-sensory' is non-existent as though natural phenomena were limited to our powers of perceiving them. It is therefore pertinent to quote an eminent scientist, Sir Alan Parkes, on the subject of the honey bee which 'navigates, finds water, estimates fuel consumption and communicates with other individuals by means which would be incredible if they were not scientifically demonstrable. A human being who suddenly acquired perceptions of this kind would certainly be written off as fraudulent.'[25]

It seems very probable (to say the least) that only a tiny fraction of natural phenomena are perceived by man. We are prisoners of our own conception of space, as a volume which contains nothing which we cannot detect, but it is already clear that space which is probably infinite, not volumetric, can be permeated by many things which we cannot perceive and there is no reason why, even if there is such a thing as measurable space (that is to say enclosed volume apprehensible by us) it should not 'contain' a great variety of coincident but unconnected chains of happening just as easily as it 'contains' a weird variety of television programmes.

The old religions were definitive and exceedingly crude. Man, as he now is, varies from the very primitive idolator to the modern man capable of thinking scientifically and philosophically.[26] Religion likewise varies from the primitive to the sophisticated but the principal religions available are run by priests who naturally cater for the majority of their customers. A few of these priests are capable of transcending the average level and it would appear that religion, if it really were to abandon superstition and corrupt subservience to lower levels of intellect, apprehension and education, could proceed along the same lines as science towards a greater and truer knowledge of the nature of what we call God.

It is not enough to pretend that God does not exist because we create him in our own thoughts. Does he exist in us or we in him? Who first uttered the Word? It is a profound mystery but it does exist as a challenge. It does not disappear by pretending it does not exist.

We 'made God in our own image' because we knew no better and it is easy to be facetious about this but the fundamental problem, well stated in *Genesis,* remains. *The earth was without form and void—and God said.* Wherever we probe it the world is *with* form, It has shape and reason and consistence as though someone had willed it, designed it. In what way, and in what sense this can be true we cannot say, but if we can abandon the primitive fantasies of a father-god and explore the means that are open to us for communion, we may find that man's instinct for religion is well founded in nature.

It is an outrageous conceit that Earth is the religious centre of the universe and most religions as generally practised are only one step up from the idea of a tribal god. But the idea of God as the totality of the existence of the universe is tremendous.

Spiritual experience is sufficiently well attested to be worthy of serious investigation. Meanwhile the better among the old kinds of religion may continue to serve a useful purpose. Any way into a spiritual experience of the universe, as distinct from a physical or intellectual apprehension of it, is an enrichment of life, even if it is a corrupt way in, but we must hope for great progress in religion amounting to a transformation. Negation is not enough.

A man's religion is his relationship with God. It is the reasonable belief of many people that a good relationship with God will be reflected in a good life but it is illogical to argue that because a man leads a good life (one of which we approve) his relationship to God, that is his religious life, is also satisfactory. It is the sad experience of many worthy people and practising Christians that they have never had a religious experience in their lives whereas some 'sinners' have felt themselves very close to God. Jesus (who of course was not a Christian), seems, in the reports which we have of what he taught, to have been occasionally confused but generally remarkably clear in his distinction between religion and morality, though aware of a relationship between the religious life of a man and his behaviour as a citizen. But being a Jew, brought up in a pious Jewish home and taught the scriptures, even though he was outstandingly critical and free-thinking, Jesus was bound to have been conditioned to the scriptural idea of *sin,* announced in *Genesis* and pervading the whole of the Old Testament. His marvellous response was to preach forgiveness.

Religion is not about sin: it is about spiritual experience. Spiritual experience may be achieved or enhanced by spiritual exercises such as prayer, or by being in special places. Spiritual experience may be thought to imply the existence of God but this may not be so. It rather depends upon what we mean by God. It would be very foolish in the present state of ignorance to attempt to define God. It is also foolish to deny the possible existence of something which has been attested by experience but which cannot be defined.

If religious life is to be sustained in communities it needs organization, just as hospitals, drama and music need organization, to survive and develop but it should be clear that the function of religious societies, such as churches, is to foster the religious life of their members not to legislate for their moral behaviour. The danger of churches is that human beings, by their nature, are almost incapable of refraining from disapproval and moral intervention in the lives of others. It needs the kind of spiritual experience which came to Jesus to make it clear that they must not do this and, unfortunately, this is the kind of experience which seldom comes the way of clergy and the dignitaries of any human organization.

In the field of religion we are profoundly ignorant and awkward. If religion is the relationship between individual experience of life and the totality of existence it is something we need to explore.

Chapter Fourteen

THE ROLE OF POLITICS

As ARISTOTLE observed, 'man is by nature a political animal'.[27] He has to live in communities but as man, distinguished from the other animals, he needs more than herd instinct and evolved behaviour patterns. He has language by which to communicate ideas as a result of which he has become argumentative. It seems to be a part of his nature to seek to improve his lot instead of accepting it, as other animals do, and this will to improve has been one of the principal reasons why he has become the dominant species on Earth. Apparently no other species has the will to improve and it is one of the most remarkable of natural phenomena that man is thus equipped with an urge to change his condition rather than to survive in it. Man is an ameliorating animal, a dissatisfied animal, a force let loose upon the face of Earth which has an active will towards improvement. It is because of this sense of a mission to improve that man has to be a political animal.

At the present stage of human development politics are even more discredited than religion in public opinion and the reasons are similar. Politics have failed to keep pace with modern needs, have failed to adapt to the conditions of a world enlightened by science as a way of thinking.

At first glance public opinion may seem to be a very poor standard by which to judge the failure of politics or religion. It is notoriously ill-informed, prejudiced, cruel, venal and dreary; but we cannot escape from our nature which demands that we live in communities which have a will towards the improvement of their lot, and upon their success as communities in a competitive world depends their future survival. Some social groups fail and despite great merits they are extinguished, sometimes with appalling agony. Others stagnate and remain for perhaps centuries—nature does not watch the clock—potential failures or successes. Others go ahead, sometimes towards success and sometimes towards disaster.

The medium in which the politician works is public opinion, the will of the effective majority, just as an artist works in paint and a composer of music in modulated sound. The word *effective* is important, indeed crucial to the argument. The will to improve which distinguishes man, is variable, stronger in some people than others and perhaps generally stronger in men than in women. Nature seems to have arranged that those who must bring up children and survive at all costs should be adaptable to conditions whereas the men, who are not essential once they have fertilized the egg, and who are genetically over-abundant, seem to be endowed with the natural responsibility to progress. On the other hand, the female, being the bearer of the next generation, is the natural gad-fly of her husband, urging him to better things. It is all rather primitive but this is the way we are!

Because some people, men and women, are supine and many are gullible, the effective majority, the people who affect the political destiny of a community, may well be a minority of the total population. At the very lowest level there are those in a democratic community who do not use their vote but they are joined by some, at what might be called the highest level, who refrain from voting, not because of lack of interest but because there is no party which can command their respect. This upper minority may contain the best and most creative people in the community.

The politician operates upon the politically active central

section of the community and his aim is to advance the interests of the community with the assent of the majority of this section. Below it the supine component is politically inactive and above it the creative minority is forming the pattern of the next political generation or exploring unviable alternatives. In politics the viable, that is what can be done, is limited to what can be understood and supported by the majority of those who take an interest in the development and progress of the community. The size of this politically important element in society varies very much according to the opportunities, traditions and educational facilities of the society. In some social groups autocracy flourishes because it is the only active element in the population. In other societies progress is inhibited because the active element completely frustrates the creative minority. This is the particular danger of socialist societies, whereas the stagnation of autocratic societies results from the frustration of the participation of the majority.

The worst that can happen to any political community is that it becomes dominated by the section of the community which does not want change. The next worst is that it becomes dominated by the aristocracy or oligarchy which resists change except insofar as it accords with their own interest. The norm of human organization is that there is a central majority which generally believes in betterment but has to be convinced, which does not originate but does decide, because it has the weight of numbers. It is possible to argue that the creative minority should have the political power but the creative minority is seldom if ever united in its opinions and, in any case, could not exist in isolation, so *the central body of accessible but uncommitted opinion is a necessary element in politics of any flavour.* Dictatorships, we should remind ourselves, come into being and can only exist by public consent. Once established, however, a dictatorship can take active steps to increase, mainly through fear and partly by deprivation of opportunity, the supine element in the population and it can exterminate the creative minority.

Thus it seems clear that one of the hazards to which any community is prone is the danger of dictatorship which will, in the end, having satisfied the personal desires of the ruling junta, destroy or cripple the political viability of the community as compared with other communities. The essence of dictatorship is to convince the political medium (the majority) that it is politically insignificant. It thus depoliticalizes the community and renders it virtually uncompetitive though it probably maintains that it is doing the exact opposite.

Politics is 'the art of the possible' and in the long run depends upon convincing the convincible and potentially active middle section of the population towards a particular course of action or way of life.

As with morality there is no guarantee that any political theory or system is *right*. The test in politics is, immediately whether it is possible, intermediately whether it works and long term whether it succeeds in terms of improving the standard of living of the community.

The development of communism is typical. It began with the ideas of a creative minority. It was established by an effective majority of those who were open to conviction and disposed to action. It proceeded by the destruction of opposition and presently it subsists by the enlargement of the supine element at the disposal of the active element. Unless human experience throughout evolution is to be reversed, a new, thinking but uncreative central body will arise ready to exert its irresistible weight against what has become an isolated and uncreative minority. On the edge of the central majority a new creative minority will grow. This is the way it has usually been, but some communities have had the misfortune to develop a situation out of which there was no escape except death.

The law of life is change and adaptation. Every political

concept for which permanence is claimed is either a fatal liability or it is due for replacement. In the, on the whole rather sad, history of mankind the domination of a change-resisting establishment leading to social atrophy and apathy has been all too common. The spectacular rise of western civilization, against the background of human stagnation elsewhere, is due to western man's ability to fight for and retain freedom of choice, to resist tyrannical systems and believe in the peculiar quality of man as an animal with a built-in urge to improve himself.

If politics is the means by which man finds out the limits of what is possible in the direction which is thought to be progress, and if the art is directed, no matter how misguidedly, towards the betterment of the human condition, why has politics, like religion, sunk in public esteem? After all it is the art of exploiting public estimation.

As with religion the reasons are simple and valid. Politics has always offered opportunities and therefore attracted dishonest men. Modern politics is very dishonest in societies where science has established higher standards of truth which challenge the validity of politics. It is a very curious fact of modern life that science can only proceed from truth to truth and cannot prosper on any basis of deliberate falsehood, whereas religion has ardently defended obvious lies, and politics has a method of procedure which does not propagate truth or genuine understanding nor does it seek honestly for the most satisfactory solution.

For democratic politics the root of evil lies in the system of debate. One does not arrive at the best answer by discussing a motion that *this house believes this rather than that,* and allowing the speakers on each side of the house to state the case for their point of view and ignore the case against. We have the same antiquated procedure in our law courts and in industrial relations. Instead of men of good will sitting down together to find out the *truth* we have in our courts, a counsel for the prosecution and a counsel for the defence, neither of whom is concerned with the truth; both of whom may be committed to argue for something they do not believe in because the truth may well, and often does, lie somewhere between or even outside the evidence they produce and the arguments they use. The procedure of the union debate would rightly be regarded as ridiculous in the solution of any problem which came within the purview of scientific investigation. It belongs to the past and so does the political system of parties which stems from it. Over a very wide sector of human problems, which are essentially political problems, the system of party debate does not produce sensible answers nor does it ensure adequate action. Problems are not considered on their merits, on the facts, on the evidence, or on their social implications but on their relationship to the party line. Even if the parties were conducted with strict honesty, which they are not, this would be an absurd way of finding out the best way of proceeding under given conditions.

We also have the problem of democracy. The word means rule by the people but the term *people* (*demos*) may vary in its meaning from the original Greek concept (and they invented the word democracy) of the leading citizens who were sufficiently educated and experienced to have valuable opinions, to the mass democracy of everyone over eighteen having a vote.

If we look dispassionately at the nature of man, as an ameliorating animal, we may well conclude that mass democracy has fewer disadvantages than any other system but cleavage on party lines is an absurdity. Probably the great majority of voters approve some of the policies of one party and some of the policies of another. Neither satisfies them. They may, for example, believe that a social democratic party is right in promoting a greater degree of social equality and at the same time think that nationalization of industry is a mistake. They may believe that the protection of private property is in the long-term interests of the nation and at the same time think that there should be more foot-paths between youth hostels. They may believe that the preservation of historic buildings is important and find that any of the parties for which they might vote are unlikely to provide the necessary funds for preservation.

The political systems are out of tune with the times, out of tune with an educated people who want things to be *discussed on their merits*, out of tune with a society which believes that politics should not be used for personal aggrandisement.

We learn at school how to look at a problem and try to find the right answer. We are taught and believe that truth is the basis of knowledge, that progress depends upon respect for truth in science and all that stems from science, which means most of industry and the way we earn our living; but in politics we are still stuck with the old rules of debate under which respectable men deny the truth and suppress the truth in parliament and in the law courts because they believe, sincerely but misguidedly, in the antiquated notion that the rules of debate lead to a discovery of the truth. In fact they are an antiquated, nonsensical game only fit for children who have been to a not very good school.

Underlying the distrust of the system of politics is distrust of the people who go into politics. It is justified and we should consider this in relation to our thoughts about the work standard (Chapter 8). We need a radical overhaul so that it is possible for quite a lot of honest men, men of integrity, to participate in politics.[28] The system has gone rotten and it must be put right if we are to survive. Let us not pretend that by acquiescence and shrugging our shoulders, when the local lad uses the system to become a millionaire, we can escape responsibility or the consequences. If the political system of a country fails the country will fail.

But it is not only on the political level that our problems can be solved. Politics is concerned with what the community as a community wants to do, the way it wants to organize itself and, ultimately, with what degree of freedom indivi-

duals in the community are to enjoy and what the community
—'they'—can do to the individual.

It is worth saying that the proper role of government is to
facilitate. But in the interests of well-being, which is what
politics is really about, the most important single thing is to
preserve the power of the talented individual, the unusual,
non-average, creative person, to make his contribution and
leaven the lump.

The challenge of this is to every individual to ask whether
he is part of the lump. It is not a question of being original
and famous but of making a contribution above the ordinary.
In effect this usually means, at present, doing one's job
rather well. In many situations it is more important to do
well than to do good.

Politics are important because they affect our practical
well-being, and, if we are not careful, may curtail the freedom which is necessary; but we must not expect too much of
politics. As at present conducted they are a very clumsy and
ineffectual tool and they do not attract those people who
could be most useful in politics. It is a symptom of disease
that many of the people in politics are deservedly contempt-
ible but they must be replaced. Politics is an essential part
of human activity but cannot solve all our problems. One of
our troubles in this century has been the expectation that all
our problems *could* be resolved by political means. This is
not true. Much depends upon the quality of our own way of
living, upon *ourselves* and not just upon 'them'.

It is probably true to say that we—as a community—get
the politics we deserve. But we as individuals may suffer
severely, even to death, if we belong to a community which
deserves a corrupt and vicious political set-up. We have been
encouraged to think of ourselves as individuals, not as heirs
to the sins of our fathers, but if we are not responsibility-
sharing individuals we may well become expendable com-
modities.

We may not like politics but we are animals who need

politics and we should personally care about politics just as we care about our food. They are not unrelated. Politics is the necessary art of doing things together.

The general nature of the problem seems to be to devise new institutions which will facilitate the responsible and active participation of individuals at many levels. Unfortunately the growth of population and growth in the scale of organizations is tending dangerously in the opposite direction and creating a large central section of the population which feels that it is politically sterilized. This is a very dangerous condition.

Chapter Fifteen

BETTERMENT

In THINKING about politics we have had to face the fact that man must strive for improvement. This has been his evolutionary winning characteristic. He is an ameliorating animal. But this raises the question which has been in the background from the beginning of this book, namely what is *better*? It is not just a matter of opinion; it is a fundamental convincement, indeed something even more important than that, a built-in knowledge that betterment is possible irrespective of any opinion as to what is better or worse, what is good or bad. Just as the swallow knows that it must fly north in the spring and south for the winter so man knows he must strive for improvement. This is over and above the sexual urge to reproduce and survive. He must have more than that. He must feel that he is 'getting somewhere'. We think of the rabbit as being a higher form of life than the slug, the dog higher than the rabbit, the man higher than the dog. We think we see a pattern in nature whereby species evolve, improve and survive, or fail to adapt and decline or disappear. It is part of our nature to believe in ascent.[29] Part of the trouble with us at the present time is doubt about the possibility of further ascent but at the same time we are exploring space, reaching out into the universe. This is characteristic of us.

It is arguable that man should try to change his nature but to do so would seem to mean that he would become like the other animals only cleverer in some respects. But it is questionable whether without the urge to go forward he could survive. There are societies in which effort is minimal but it is not negligible, and if one looks under the surface of such societies, one sees that mere survival is enormously difficult. To get water, to grow crops, to cut wood with primitive means absorbs immense personal effort. If we let go, if we lose faith in progress we slip back, not to effortless ease but to menial labour and stark impoverishment. We are a species that depends upon its momentum. We go forward or perish. This is the criterion of success in most of our activities. In any action which involves decision there is the possibility of making a mistake, a mistake which may prove immediately fatal or may only reveal itself after many years. The decisions we make tend to be based upon intelligent appraisal of the outcome of future action. To each of us life comes as a challenge in one form or another and the challenge has to be met by decision and by action. Such decisions and such actions are often taken instinctively but we believe that the instinctive response is *right* in most cases, and where we have to stop and think we ask ourselves what is the right thing to do. Theoretically we may be unable to distinguish right and wrong, to say which is which in any absolute sense, but in practice we know that there is a distinction and we have to work towards the right. This is more a matter of physiology than of ethics. If we balance on a log we can walk across a ravine: if we don't, we fall to our death. One can reach a state of mind when it seems right to do this and we do it because it seems right, but generally we don't fall off the log because we believe it is wrong to do so. If we do fall we fall deliberately or because we lose our nerve. It seems that, at the present time many people have at least in part lost their nerve. A possible reason for this may be that there are too many of us, because it has been observed that similar phenomena occur in animal communities when they become over-populated. (p. 21 and note 3)

Leaving aside the neurotic condition of loss of faith in living, we exist by faith in ourselves and our power to make right decisions. Relatively primitive people seem to have few doubts and act instinctively but, as man becomes more sophisticated and understands more of the implications of problems and actions, decision becomes more difficult, yet he still believes, when cogitating about a course of action, that it is possible to make a right decision or a wrong decision, and an important point to notice is that morality does not come into this assessment. The swallow does not fly south in late summer because it is morally right to do so, it goes because it is right in quite a different and unmoral way. It is right because it is *necessary*. With the swallow there does not seem to be any scope for choice: the time comes and the swallow goes. But with men there are many decisions which have to be consciously taken involving choice among two or more possibilities of action. Sometimes the preferred choice is painful, even fatal, but necessary. This kind of rightness is achieved by judgment of what is necessary or the best thing to do. Obviously it will be motivated, influenced by our desires, our character, our training, our morality, our religion, possibly our meanness or greed or jealousy; but whatever the motivation there is a faith that it is possible to make a right decision. Whether it is a good decision is quite another matter and, as in a game of snakes and ladders we are back to square one! We can either give up or throw the dice again and upon each decision to throw the dice we move one way or the other, up or down. Our object, as in life, is to go up and going back is failure. There is somewhere in this a glimpse, if no more, of one kind of rightness. At the lower levels it is instinctive and necessary for survival. As we move up it becomes more difficult but it consists in an assessment of what we are and what we want to be, what our obligations are and our interests, and the concept we have of what we are and want to be. The basis for decision may be very complex and difficult but there is the belief, which is inherent in human nature, that there is a right decision, a *better* thing to do.

We believe in right without knowing what it is. Reasoning cannot get us very far but if we look at life in the manner of an artist we may find another basis. If you begin to play the hymn 'Oh Come all ye Faithful' on the note A, the next note is A then E below, then A then B. This is a pattern which was invented by a man[30] who felt this sequence of notes. If you were composing, instead of playing, a tune you would invent a sequence which seemed to have an inner rightness, one note leading to another. You would see alternative arrangements and reject or accept until you had fashioned the tune in a way that seemed right to you. Similarly in a poem or a painting there is a rightness which belongs to the whole thing which you are creating, and there are wrongnesses which are rejected because they don't fit. All artists are familiar with this sense of rightness within the little world of the work they are doing, the object they are creating whether it is a symphony or a vase. And many artists, especially composers of music, do work within a scaffolding of rules and accepted devices.

As in a work of art, our lives consist of constant decision making, each decision being affected by what has been done, and our concept, vague or clear, of what we want to make of our lives. As artists in living we must have a *sense*, a feeling for what fits and what does not, for what would spoil the picture and what would be consistent with it. This is what we can call an *aesthetic rightness* because aesthetic is the word we derive from the ancient Greek word for feeling. This is not a matter of conscience, though artists under the influence of morality can make it a matter of conscience to do what they feel to be artistically right.

If we look at human communities we see that it is necessary for people to be different. The community requires for survival and success people with different skills, talents and temperaments. There are many different jobs to be done.

Genetically also it requires different stocks, partly in order to ensure variety and adaptability. In the stage of civilization which we have reached it is fairly commonly possible for people to decide what sort of life they want to live and what its qualities are to be. It is, more than ever before, possible to regard one's life in an aesthetic way, not in a merely utilitarian way.

If we admit that it is possible, and even desirable, to consider the *quality* of one's living by aesthetic standards it may be useful to look for a moment at the experience of artists, not in the living of life but in the practice of art. The artist, it must be remembered, is an artist in paint, or sculpture, or music and not necessarily very good at making a work of art of his own life. Sometimes his concentration upon the wholeness of his art makes an apparent disaster of his life. But if life itself can be considered artistically what are the lessons of art which might be applied to the living of it?

There are no universal laws but most artists agree that a successful work of art is consistent and complete within itself so that nothing could be added or taken away without disadvantage. Few works of art achieve this condition completely. There is an element of controlled design in all valid works of art, a logical inner structure and it is interesting to compare the work of a real artist with the therapeutic painting of a schizophrenic patient where this sense of design is often terrifyingly lacking. There is the sense of proportion which is a remarkable feeling which men have for the proper relationship of things. This is evidenced, of course, in the human body where any undue distortion of the proper relationship of the parts is liable to seem horrible. The basis of proportion is partly functional—what works well—but not entirely. Many artists would say that their work expresses feeling: not just their own feelings about themselves and their problems but, especially in great works of art, feeling which is not particular to themselves but generalized and perhaps common to all humanity.

If the artist can work by learning to translate his feeling and his intuition into a work of art so can man fashion his life upon similar principles but, if art is any guide, nothing of quality is likely to be achieved without trouble, without learning and without concentration of sometimes extreme effort comparable with climbing a difficult mountain.

The quality of life, like the quality of art comes, not from what is got out of it but what is put in, and here, we have a valuable clue to the fundamental nature of living.

Chapter Sixteen

RELATIONSHIPS—THE COMMUNITY TO THE INDIVIDUAL

S O F A R we have considered a number of separate aspects of living but nothing exists in isolation and the relationships between things are just as important as the things themselves. It is a fundamental property of matter that it *exists* by virtue of relationships between particles. This fact is demonstrated in the explosion of an atomic bomb whereby the relationships between the particles which make up an atom are broken and the energy released. Here is an obviously impressive example of the importance of relationships which, in fact, runs right through nature. Much of the confusion that exists in our thought about ourselves and the problems of living has arisen because people have isolated 'subjects of study' and thought about them without considering them in relation to other subjects of study. This separation grows upon us at school where we move from one class to another, from arithmetic to French, from physics to biology, from history to geography and it is not surprising if we fail to develop our powers of relating these subjects to each other. Thus we fail to develop the power of *significantly bringing together* and do not sufficiently realize that the study of relationships between things will reveal truths which are not apparent in the things themselves. It is an important aspect of all knowledge that the sum is more than the parts,[31] that relationships are more important than incidents. Much of the bigotry, intolerance and ruthlessness in the world is due to isolation of knowledge and ideas from the context in which they will be worked out, in other words, to neglect of relationships.

It is, however, very difficult to study relationships rather than isolated subjects and the more difficult the subjects become, as knowledge of them increases, the more difficult it is to know enough to consider any subject relatively. In this matter our educational system needs fundamental modification so that it builds bridges instead of isolated towers of thought and knowledge. Such a breakthrough in education is bound to be resisted and ridiculed by those who are stuck in the present system but it seems to be coming and it is a necessary prerequisite for the further development of civilization.

Our education, and our habits of thought, put blinkers on us so that it is not by any means easy to get a composite understanding of our problems, but we do have an apprehension of the nature of the universe which is different from what our ancestors believed to be the truth. For one thing it is very much larger than they thought it was; but when we ask, how big, there is no satisfactory answer. Both time and size are concepts which become less and less valid as we cast our thoughts towards outer space, and the progress of astro-physics has deepened the mystery not eliminated it. In many other fields of science it is also true that greater knowledge has brought awareness of the limits of our understanding at the same time as it has sharpened our understanding within the limits. In using the word *limits* we should avoid thinking of boundary fences. It is more like looking into a mist and the limits are to our powers of perception. If our eyes were sensitive to seeing reflected infra-red rays we should see further through the mist but still there would be limits. Great progress has been made in the development of instruments for looking into and exploring space but it now seems to be certain that, no matter how far the limits may be pushed back, there will always be a beyond.

Some children used to be told at school that infinity is very difficult to conceive. This is a hangover from the mechanical thinking of the nineteenth century when the world was often described as though it was a machine, but now the idea of infinity is much easier because we live in an electronic age. We are learning to discard mechanistic models for our thinking and to understand that the idea of a world with a boundary round it and 'nothing' beyond the boundary is nonsensical. Time and space, dimensions and weight, are essentially concepts of local significance to Earth. An astronaut can walk weightless in space at a known distance from Earth, but further out our concepts of time and distance become increasingly confused and it becomes fairly easy for us to think of infinity as 'going on for ever'; but this phrase really implies motion, time and distance which are all earth-bound concepts. We have at least achieved a greater sense of mystery. For one thing there are now obvious limitations to the scientific experimental method though the habit of truth which has grown from science is of universal value. Indeed I think it is true to say that science has graduated from being a quest for true knowledge into a new faith in truth as a value, in truth as such.

It is now commonplace to ask, as of right, what is the truth. It is commonplace to reject with contempt what is provenly untrue. This is an immense and incalculably powerful new force let loose among men and it cuts across most of the established procedures of politics and religion. Rulers of Church and State, to give them their due, have often been concerned with what they believed to be good but have habitually suppressed truth in the interests of what they wanted to do 'with good intentions'. Thus humbug proliferated within the portals of the church and the town hall, the police station, the parliament house and the palace of nations. The new habit of asking for and expecting the truth is a fundamental change which we owe to science. It gives a new dimension to freedom and provides a new basis for it. It has the great advantage that, over a wide spectrum of human affairs, it is possible to establish what is true and what is false, whereas it is much more difficult to be objective about what is 'good'. We are, at the same time, dependent and independent. As individuals we are islands but we cannot survive alone. We have to create communities and these seem to acquire an existence of their own, but although the community has an existence in its own nature it is an epiphenomenon[32] of many individual people. Without them it ceases to exist.

The community exists for individuals not for itself for it does not indeed have a *self*. To give it a self would be to make it into a god. The community is not a god. It has no authority. It has no physical existence except in the individuals who compose it and its nature changes with its composition. It outlasts individuals but is always made up of individuals. Its quality depends upon and varies with the quality of the people who compose it.

The danger of a community is that it may be manipulated by individuals in their own interests or, even more dangerously, in accord with some political theory, religion or creed. It then becomes an instrument of oppression, no matter how good the creed. In our time the greatest peril lies in the substitution of the State for God. Having argued that God does not exist we let in a more primitive form of god by the back door in giving selfhood—an independent existence—to *The State*. This is a step backwards because the state is, from the point of view of the individual, neutral. It exists for itself and is thus a monster.

It is also an idol. It demands the sacrifice of the individual just as primitive gods demanded sacrifice of the individual.

Man does not live for self. He has a sense of community, is friendly and capable of love. He is at his best when he is free to contribute what he feels is valuable in him to the good of the community. At the present time many people feel that they are not free to do this and we have, in fact, lost a great deal of the freedom which was painfully achieved by our ancestors. We have abolished old evils by accepting, blindly, new constraints. The purpose of government is to facilitate the development of the individual. By developing the full capacity of the individuals in it the community benefits. The state exists for people, not people for the state.

In order to have freedom within a community there must be rules and the danger of all rules is that they inhibit freedom but so, even more, does the absence of rules. The need for rules increases with the irresponsibility of individuals. An irresponsible minority can impose severe restriction upon the majority. The majority are therefore tempted to repress all minorities on the ground that all minorities are irresponsible, which is quite untrue. The progress of a community depends more than anything else upon the contribution which exceptional individuals or groups of individuals can make. The dominance of the average slows up or inhibits progress and crime—truly irresponsible behaviour—becomes a principal obstacle to freedom.

Bearing in mind that the object of government is to facilitate, and the aim of governors must be to foster the efforts of men more talented than themselves, it becomes important to legislate against actions which impair the freedom of others. Thus murder, rape, arson, theft, vandalism, rowdyism, perjury, scandal etc. all need to be prevented. They are irresponsible in that they are selfish and do harm to other people without doing any good. But it must be possible to act responsibly as an individual in the interests of the community without being a criminal. Such action must however conform to certain standards and not participate in crime. For example throwing a bomb into a café may be actuated by a genuine desire for political reform and more freedom but it is criminal because it involves murder and murder is not excusable in a civilized community. If it were, anyone would be entitled to murder in accordance with his own convictions and this will not work.

The workability of the rules of a society is something which has to be considered in a practical way and it is bound to vary from place to place. This is desirable and if we could get away from the idea of competitive national powers which has reached its extreme, and one hopes ultimate development, in our time, there would be many advantages in breaking down all organization into small communities which could be very different from each other and thus enrich the opportunities of life. The smaller community is more susceptible to the influence of individuals. Its one disadvantage is that it risks survival in a power-dominated world.

Historically, experience seems to show that life is best and richest in city states and since international war must be avoided there is really no sense in the big power groupings. The object of big groupings is simply power but already they are proving to be a straitjacket. The biggest powers are the least satisfactory in terms of quality of living, among the advanced countries, because by their bigness and impersonality they deny many of the freedoms which men want, in particular the freedom to be heard.

We need to give a great deal of thought to organising our communities at the right size and in the right ways to achieve the best opportunities for improving the quality of living. There cannot be complete freedom for the individual and there must not be complete domination by the state, but the maximum of freedom and the minimum of control is the balance to be aimed at and it involves the creation of a situation in which individuals not only can, but will and must, accept responsibility.

It is a measure of our present political degradation that we tend to think organization must increasingly supplant individual responsible initiative. An appalling result of this is that initiative is taken away from the naturally creative, inventive, lively minds and transferred to the kind of people who like to work in municipal offices and the civil service.[13] Much of the trouble which we experience is due to the sheer size of the administrative units and we need to study much more effectively the relationship between size and real efficiency, bearing in mind that the object of good government must be to maximize the contribution made by the individual and increase his opportunities. The enlargement of administrative units beyond a certain point (well below the size of a national government department or a nationalized industry) seems to have the reverse effect. Here is a case where we particularly need to shed the blinkers of political theory and look for the truth about what does work in human terms and what does not.

It would be presumptuous here to attempt to deal in detail with the questions of how big communities should be and how they should be governed. It is however of vital importance that people should think a great deal about these things and that the present creaking, inefficient political systems all over the world should be replaced by arrangements which will facilitate good government. I suspect that size is a crucial factor and confidence in peace a prerequisite of sensible government. The price we pay for allowing international arguments to be settled by the criminal practice of war is much greater even than the enormous sums we waste upon the production of armaments.

If we were able to settle down and work out sensible arrangements for the government of communities we should expect, not to establish a standard method but to create a great variety of organizations according to the needs and conditions of various communities. We should also expect to achieve what might be called multi-dimensional systems. We have these to some extent already in the stratification of international organizations concerned with particular aspects such as health and trade. The old national boundaries are a nuisance in terms of government and good administration but they have their value culturally and socially in breaking down the mass of humanity into coherent societies. In the case of the larger countries there is a need for more subdivision such as home rule for Scotland and the re-establish-ment of the provinces of France. Nations should only exist in the cultural and social sense. At the same time some aspects of government need to be administered on a larger scale than at present and it would be helpful if we could develop the idea of limited sovereignty. In this way a complex tissue of overlapping and interlocking areas of government would emerge. But it would be unsuitable here to digress into a detailed consideration.

The main objective should be to achieve political organiza-tions which will facilitate the development of individual human qualities, and this means, not uniformity but a great variety of social environments with freedom of movement among them. The aim should be to foster creative relation-ships and so to enrich not standardize experience.

Chapter Seventeen

RELATIONSHIPS—THE INDIVIDUAL TO THE COMMUNITY

U NDOUBTEDLY WE can find fulfilment in devoting ourselves in part to the good of the community, in being public
spirited, in accepting responsibilities, in adding in one way
or another to the richness of communal life, but we do so
out of our own choice though probably influenced by
fashion. All of us, to some extent, depend for the quality of
our own lives, for our happiness and self respect, upon our
relationship with other people and what they think of us.
Because the community is made up of changing individuals,
some of whom may affect it more than others, its character
varies and it is also subject to influences from outside. We
are aware, at the present time, of tides in fashion which
come like winds of unknown origin and our behaviour, our
attitudes to other people, our evaluations are quite strongly
affected by them.

The origins of fashions in feeling would make a very
interesting study and it would be possible to know a great
deal more about them. There are times when rudeness and
toughness are admired, as they have been recently, and this
may well be because the trend of society has been away
from conditions in which toughness and violence could possibly be effective. There is a nostalgic longing for quick,
violent solutions which are in fact impossible unless modern
society is to commit suicide. There are already signs of a
new and more realistic fashion for gentleness, for manners
and for courtesy. People are beginning to appreciate flowers

and decoration afresh and there is a great need for *a new tenderness*. Toughness may represent the last convulsion of the old world. It is mainly found among those who are failing to adapt to new conditions in which mental finesse and emotional sensitivity are increasingly necessary.

We take some of our character from our environment. There is something of the chameleon in all of us but the essential self is unique and often rather lonely. Loneliness is, paradoxically, often the result of expecting too much from other people and giving too little out of oneself. There is a tendency to think that the quality of one's personal life is dependent upon outside factors, upon the love of other people, upon friends, upon opportunities, upon money but in fact it is mainly dependent upon oneself.

Man is a new element in nature because he has imagination. He is creative. He can conceive what does not exist. This could be what lies behind the creation legend (*Genesis I 27*) that God created man in his own image; not a physical image, which is absurd, but able to create as nothing else in nature can create because only man, so far as we know, has the power of imagination and the faculty to use it.

The natural outcome of creativity is love. The fulfilment of one's nature would seem to be in doing what one is especially equipped by nature to do and in the case of man it is to love. But we misunderstand the meaning of that word. Love is not possession but the exercise of *the faculty to give creatively*.

> *If love be not creative is it true?*
> *For love is giving and creates to give,*
> *Enjoins the lover outside self to live,*
> *Not passively accept, nor yet pursue*
> *To gain, possess nor mutual comfort take.*
> *Contentment is not love, indeed there's pain.*
> *Love serves as no man's tool and asks no gain;*
> *But I'll not grant that love can be to make*

The best of failure, patiently to bear
The brunt of life. Though noble that is less
Love is far more than service, more than care,
Though these are good and born of kindliness.
Love is a force creating life and beauty,
A tender dedication not a duty.[34]

The nature of love is concern for and involvement in someone else or some other people, and to be at the receiving end of love is very pleasant. So much is this so that many people ruin their own lives for lack of other people's love. But love is not to be constrained, commanded nor required. It is or it is not. We have no right to it but we need to give it. This is the real nub of the problem and those people who languish for lack of love, as they see it, are misconceiving its nature. Love is not receptive; it is creative and outward-going. If this is understood much of the wise teaching of the Christian gospel fits into the pattern of modern life.

But what if we give and are rebuffed? What if we find that our love, expressed, for example, in the willingness to serve the common good, is rejected? The immediate question is whether what we have had to offer was good enough. Suppose we felt the gift of painting in us and found nobody who would exhibit our pictures the answer could well be that they were trite and of no value to others though we gained satisfaction from doing them. Love should imply modesty. We are much beguiled by the urge to *express ourselves* in order to make our mark upon society. This is like the cowboy who put a notch upon his gun for every man he killed. It is nothing to do with love.

Nor is possession compatible with love. Love is pure giving, not taking. Nor is it required to be limited to one person for that is not its nature. To expect to monopolize the love of anyone is to seek to diminish their stature, to deprive them of the capacity to grow in creative relationships with other people.

Many men and women experience love at least for a short time when they 'fall in love' but this is a complicated psychophysical condition.[35] The essence of love is the absence of desire, not the gratification of it. Desire should be recognized for what it is, a part of our nature, the basic drive to reproduce, but not love.

For practical purposes it might be better to avoid the confusing and ambiguous word love and simply say that the relationship of an individual towards the community, which is made up of his fellow men, should be open, generous and responsible: he should wish to give and be entitled to respect for giving. The community, as we have seen, is not an entity in its own right; it is made up of individuals. It is a simple fact of life that if the individuals work together in a generous and creative way they improve their own lot as individuals. If people try to take more out than they put in, the community is weakened and they themselves participate in the communal impoverishment. It is really very simple and obvious. It is how any team works but it needs to be restated.

But a good team is not made up of a set of ignorant low-grade people. The quality depends partly upon team spirit but very largely upon the quality of the individuals who compose it. It is here that political thinking seems to go most wildly wrong. Party loyalty and fidelity to the team is useless if the individuals are of poor quality and quality in a human being depends upon the opportunity to develop it. This is a personal matter and fine human beings are not produced like bricks out of a slot. They have to create themselves and to do this they must have freedom.

Chapter Eighteen

SLAVE MENTALITY

M A N Y O F the obstacles to improving the quality of life are political and economic. We have considered the political problem but said little so far about economics. This is deliberate because our present economic system is chaotic and based upon a concept which needs to be questioned. That concept is that man is a working animal, a slave. Oddly enough this economic attitude did not apply in the ancient world where slavery was general. Men were divided into two categories, slaves and free. The slaves were owned as property by the free. This enabled the successful free man to live without labour and to cultivate the art of living. Work was done by the slaves. Wealth consisted of things of inherent value like land, gold, and the products of labour. The possession of working slaves was thus an element of wealth. A principal object of being wealthy was to enjoy life. It did not always work out that way but in general the lot of a slave was wretched and the privilege of freedom was to live and not to work.

With the disappearance of slavery some very strange things happened. In particular the owner of slaves was replaced by the employer of labour. The owner looked after his property but the employer was, to a large extent, relieved of the need to do this. The possession of money enabled him to exploit the former slave class, the workers, without any obligation even of self interest. For the worker to survive he had to have work, and for work he was paid. Thus most people came to consider that the whole business of living was conditioned by their right to sell their own labour and the standard of living depended upon their work (their skill, strength and the amount they could extract from the employer in exchange for their work). For the great majority of people living has become a transaction based upon their own work, and with the growth of social democracy inevitably the work standard has prevailed and people demand the *right* to work.

Modern technology is rapidly changing the nature of work. On the one hand there is less and less need for unskilled work and on the other the value of skilled work in terms of production is increasing, probably in direct proportion to the skill and knowledge of the worker. Put like this it sounds fine but the social consequences are terrifying unless we change our attitude to work. Almost certainly educational facilities are falling behind the population increase, and in any case there is a fairly high proportion of human beings whose capacity for learning is low. We can therefore envisage a new class of people for whom there will be no work and another new class, a work-aristocracy of the highly skilled (the meritocracy). This is assuming that we continue with our ridiculous system of believing that the justification of man is work. It is now a completely barbarous idea and should be scrapped.

The right of a man to live does not depend upon his ability to work. We acknowledge this to be so in most civilized communities. We provide, from community funds for the maintenance of imbeciles, sick, maimed and even criminals whom we think must be kept apart but we think the able bodied and sane should work or want. It was a bad idea but now it is an unworkable idea because there just will not be the work for everyone to do. Since world economy is based very largely upon wealth resulting from work, and in a sensible reorientation of life work would cease to be central, the discussion of current economics would be a waste of time. We need a complete rethinking of economics.

Man is not justified by what he does but by what he is. It is not true that a man is known by his works and we have to make the creative leap, from thinking which was conditioned by the necessity for work into a new way of thinking which will be suitable for a society in which there will be less work to be done in the sense that work has been understood in the past. In future the idea that a man must earn his living by his work will not work. And there is no real reason why it should. But it will be a difficult transition because many people will have to learn new attitudes to life and there is bound to be regret that the good which was brought out in people by having to work may be lost.

But if we displace work as the economic basis of life, which eventually we must, an entirely different prospect opens up. Many great men who had no need to work *for a living* did in fact work hard in a variety of ways, some in public service and some in the furtherance of private interests such as archaeology or botany. The abolition of the work standard might possibly free work from many of the restrictions which have come to impede it. There are many desirable things which used to be available but no longer are because the labour cost is too high—from personal service to craftsmanship. Economy based on work has to a large extent strangled itself and with all sorts of interesting things to be done we have created economic barriers to the doing of them. It is an idiotic economic system which bases wealth on work and frustrates work.

Sooner or later we shall have to accept the principle that every member of a community is entitled to sustenance by the community according to its means. It will then at last be possible, if we do not tie ourselves up with still more ideological restrictions, for each to contribute to the well being of the community according to his capacity. No doubt some stratification will emerge but this should happen naturally in the various communities and be worked out in different ways. Here again there is the prospect of enormous fields for experiment in the art and technique of living.

There is one obvious and major difficulty in the vast disparity between the economic conditions of the developed and the under-developed countries. The key to the door out of the old world of work or want is advanced technology applied to industry and agriculture. Years ago rich people in fine houses caught cholera from the adjoining slums and gradually it was realized that the only way to get rid of the cholera was to improve the conditions under which poor people were constrained to live. It is still true that diseases, such as influenza, build up in crowded slums and spread round the world. It is still thought, by that tough breed of men who believe that their present wealth is the just reward of their merits, that economic health and disease can be kept apart. The only solution seems to be to use the resources of the advanced countries to help the backward. It is not a question of what they deserve but what is necessary and there is no question of charity in it.

One of the most important ways in which we must help is in the limitation of population and to do this we must first set our own house in order. It is no use preaching eugenics for foreigners only.

Chapter Nineteen

SOME CONCLUSIONS

I t h a s been necessary to consider many aspects of living more or less separately and with Chapter Sixteen we began to look at the importance of relationships, thus drawing the separate threads together to some extent. We want to avoid the often repeated unwisdom of trying to reduce the complexities of living within a simple formula. The message of this book is that the glory of life must be in its variety, its complexity, its manifold opportunities for unique individuals to make their contribution to the development of man. We cannot see any end, and like a work of art each life can be conceived as providing its own justification. The tenour of our thoughts has been general and theoretical: it may be useful in this final chapter to consider a few of the implications for the individual human being faced with the problems of living in the modern world. This will involve a certain amount of repetition of what has been said in earlier chapters but in a new context.

Birth

The birth of a child is the creation of a new citizen, a new centre of individuality and responsibility. It is necessary that the child should be properly reared and this is a reasonable requirement for society to make against the parents. It is an obligation which they may not be able to fulfil because of illness or death or even because of prior claims of the community against father or mother, as happens in war, so ultimately the community may have to take responsibility for the child. This poses difficult problems which require much study but it does seem to be clear that the bringing of a child into the world is not a responsibility of the parents only but also a legitimate matter of public concern. In the past, when the survival of communities was at stake, there was some excuse for curtailing any practice which would diminish the birth rate but in the modern situation the community might reasonably require some assurance that a new citizen would be of good quality.

The conclusion seems to be that sex, as a necessary and delightful personal relationship, is a matter for individuals but conception and birth are of public concern because the quality of a community, and life in the community, are affected by the sort of people who are born into it, and the number of them.

A lamentable paradox of our thinking about liberty in the modern world is that we seem to regard sexual intercourse and the bearing of children as absolutely free but we impose massive restrictions upon the human being from the moment of being conceived. It should be the other way round. Society has a right to control the quality and quantity of its intake because the survival of the community depends upon the people who compose it, but once a child is born the contribution it can make to society depends upon the quality of environment which free individuals are free to create.

Education

Once a child is born its parents or foster parents become the link between it and the rest of the human community. Its opportunities often depend upon its parents, and so do its limitations. We generally assume that the family is the best way of bringing up children and it certainly has the advantage of peculiarity, of providing a variety of unique stimuli, but we do not really know whether other methods might be better. We have never given them a fair trial and at present the dice are loaded against the institutionally brought-up child so we do not know how well he would do in a free market, free that is from the overwhelming prejudice of the norm. There is probably a good deal of evidence, if we care to collect it, that the professional 'parents' of such institutions as the National Children's Homes and Dr. Barnardo's Homes do a better job than many 'natural' fathers and mothers. The problems of the institutional child arise, not so much from the nature of his upbringing as from popular prejudice against it, and the feed-back from prejudice to the child itself (Compare illegitimacy, p. 35) which is one of the major evils inherent in communities, and, as such, to be guarded against.

The quality of a child's education depends partly upon parents and partly upon school. There is a tendency for professional teachers to think that they do the job better but this is not always true. The educational system as we know it is largely conditioned by what government considers to be the most useful output from schools.[36] There is thus an emphasis upon conformity and minor technical skills— reading, writing and arithmetic. The advantage of parents and foster parents is that they are on the side of their individual child. A good education needs both partiality and impartiality, encouragement from those who are prejudiced in favour, as well as the impartiality of those who must try to be fair and just to all children.

Even in the most advanced countries educational systems are deplorable and generally tend to frustrate the development of real individuality but at the same time they are open to the criticism that they over-protect. In the school environment one is taught to believe that merit is rewarded. Leaving aside the big question of what is merit, this is very doubtful in the world outside. Even more peculiar is the creation of an atmosphere in which boys and girls are encouraged to develop their talents without effective challenge or opposition and it is generally understood that society, as represented by the school, is on their side. Outside school the reverse is usually the case and the most traumatic period of adjustment in a life takes place when a boy or girl leaves school to emerge from a sympathetic environment into one which is generally hostile. The fault lies with society, rather than with the schools. We expect higher standards, and different standards, in our children and their teachers from those which we exemplify in our own lives. The working out of a better society is to be seen in our better schools and the revolt of youth against 'the establishment' is a valid statement of no confidence in their elders, who are revealed hypocrites. Unfortunately the young are educated by people who are preponderantly rather dim, yet even so the children have higher ideals and a better conception of what life is about than their parents. We should be encouraging a proportion of the best brains in the community to participate in education. If we could abandon the work standard it might become, as it should be, a high privilege to be allowed to teach the young. (A contributory reason for the downfall of Roman civilization was the entrustment of education to slaves.) There is everything to be said for bringing into the schools as teachers on short term or part time commissions a variety of worthy people from outside *but* they must regard it as a privilege and they *must be prepared to undertake the necessary preparation,* probably by attending courses along with professional teachers on refresher courses. This is another case where the abandonment of the work standard would encourage greater flexibility.

The purposes of education need to be stated and at appropriate stages students should be reminded of why they are at school or college.

The first purpose is to equip the student with the skills and knowledge and the ability to work with other people which will enable him to fashion his life as well as can be expected in the present state of knowledge and the social environment as it exists.

The second purpose is to enable the student to understand and come to terms with his own nature in the context of society.

The third purpose is to develop the sense of responsibility upon which the progress of civilized life depends, as well as personal relationships.

The fourth is to provide within society people who have the skills and knowledge which are necessary. For this purpose some kind of examination system is required in order to test the capacity of the candidate for the job, but if we went off the work standard this would look very different. In the future more and more work will require skill and it should be a matter of personal pride to equip oneself to do a job and therefore welcome the opportunity of examinations.

The fifth is to give the student, and this applies especially to males, the opportunity to prove himself to himself. This is important and it is done to some extent in examinations and sport but it needs to be developed. A young man does need to prove to himself that he has guts and this cannot be done if danger is not real and challenges are artificial.[37] The reality of the challenge is probably more important than the reality of danger. There should be the opportunity in a civilized and cultivated society for testing oneself in a difficult and worth while quest. (The idea is medieval but none the worse for that because in the middle ages there was a healthy belief that a man should be a man. The principles of true knighthood are worthy of study.) The test does not necessarily require open country while we have urban jungles but organized access to wild places such as Norway and Greenland could be valuable.[38] However, the main opportunities would seem to lie with short-term apprenticeships in difficult enterprises such as road and dam building, reclamation of industrial slums, demolition, deep sea fishing, oil drilling, major building operations, surveying, forestry and social services.

The sixth is to develop courage, particularly the courage required to disagree with the majority opinion. It is essential for a healthy community that the policies of the herd should be enlightened by non-conformity.

The seventh is to encourage the development of imagination which is necessary for foresight and can provide the means of extending experience outside the inevitable limitations of a single lifetime. It is also the basis of most creative activities in science and art.

The eighth is to develop the power to think about the nature of man and the relationship of the individual to society and to the universe. This is what history and philosophy are about. The study of these is necessary if we are to generate a politically mature people. Religion comes into this but as at present taught it is too naïve and corrupt to be of much value.

The ninth, and this is closely related to the third and the eighth, is to develop a sense of proportion, of the relatedness of things, the consequences of action and of practicality.

The tenth is to foster interests outside self.

The eleventh is teaching how to manage one's own body and developing healthy habits.

The twelfth is possibly the most important; to develop a sense of respect for quality in all things and consequent humility.

An interesting question is how long should education continue. It should continue intermittently throughout life, if only as a necessary aid in adaptation to changing circumstances, but if we abandoned the work standard it would seem desirable that many people should remain students until they were at least thirty. Our present standards of graduation at twenty-one and twenty-two are widely recognized as no more than a qualification to begin serious study. If there were a personal income, irrespective of employment in work, as we now understand it, a man could remain a student all his life if he so wished, as was possible in the older university colleges until recently when they became principally places for educating the young. The object of a true student is to improve some of his own qualities, particularly qualities of mind, and society should be interested in encouraging him to do this. It is not a one way traffic but a social necessity, and the proper function of a university is not teaching but to bring the best minds of one generation into creative contact with the best minds of the next generation. People who have to be taught everything don't understand this.

Prostitution of Education

Education is commonly corrupted by being made to subserve ulterior motives of adult pressure groups. Three types of prostitution call for comment here. They are the use of education for political or religious indoctrination, as a means of social reform and as a filter for the selection of employees.

Indoctrination of any kind, being the imposition of ideas upon the immature mind with the object of making that mind conform uncritically to the creed or party which has power to impose its ideas, is the antithesis of true education. In a scientific age it is also likely to bounce back and destroy confidence in the party or church, but not before immense damage has been done and many of the minds rendered incapable of reorientation. Doctrinaire teaching, which does not envisage the inevitable changes in the climate of human thought and feeling, may be likened to a time-fuse which will have disastrous effects upon adult personality.

It is not the proper function of education to grade people. If it is necessary that they should be graded according to capacity and merit this may have to be done in schools and colleges but it is not part of education. The universities, with their adulation of the honours degree are the primary source of a corruption which has spread right back to the junior schools. This is unfortunate because the universities are also the principal upholders of the belief that study, like art, is a valuable and ennobling activity. It should however be noted that modern society has given to the originally purely academic accolade of a first class honours degree a practical significance which it was not intended to have and the pressure of numbers upon hopelessly inadequate resources in the universities of all countries has militated against the achievement of academic ideals.

Thirdly, education must not be used as a method of social levelling: that problem should be tackled, if it needs to be, at the adult level, and education must be seen as the means of giving every child and student the best chance to develop his own capacities and personality. This is bound to result in the opposite of equality and indeed the very idea of equality among people is sinister. We are not units or symbols but individuals and unique. We do not all want the same opportunities and the same kind of education.

Underlying the progressive prostitution of education is the mean doctrine of the need to be fair. 'Not fair' is the constant complaint of the lazy and incompetent. It is seldom heard from the handicapped. How can we reasonably expect life to be fair when we are all different, with different talents and needs, living in a natural environment which takes no account whatsoever of the idea of fairness? (Germs, cancer, earthquakes and, on the other side, good health, good fortune and nationality are, so far as we can judge, completely devoid of fairness.) We must believe in the rights of man and we must be honest, but to be fair in the sense in which that word is commonly used at present, is usually impossible; and when it results for example, in denying a special kind of education to one child, whose talents need it, because it would be unfair to other children who could not benefit from it, we are making fairness mean equality and thereby frustrating the essential quality of men which is their individuality that is to say, their inequality! Social justice is a noble concept but educational opportunity should be guaranteed in a just society, not made the means of achieving a just society. We have no right to enforce upon children and students the constraints of an egalitarianism which adults have not, and probably never will, accept for themselves.

It is also necessary to state that education is by no means limited to school and college. It is really something people should do for themselves, partly in educational institutions, partly at home and to a large extent by their relationship to their total environment. It is the means of becoming a mature adult.

Personal-Relationships, Growing up, Marriage

One of the conceptual dangers of our time is a morbid tendency to consider people in groups, such as race, religion, colour, educational attainment, employment, age and sex. Collaterally we have a sinister tendency of each group to attain self-awareness as a group and to aggrandize itself. Groups are easier to think about and administer than individuals, but it is all too easy to forget that all the members of the group are different individuals. Furthermore, most individuals belong to many groups, such as church, industry, trade union, women's voluntary services and so on. Thinking by groups is necessarily shallow and unnecessarily divisive.

About half the people in the world are male and the other half female. It is possible to think of this as a great division, as two groups, and the modern tendency is to argue for equality between them. The idea of equality of the sexes is just as misleading as the concept of all men being equal. Men and women are both human and under modern conditions their ways of living are much less differentiated than in the past. Each sex has special qualities in which it generally excels the other but in almost any quality the most excellent of either sex are far superior to the generality of both sexes. Even in athletics which are sports of physical prowess, devised by men for men, the women champions are far better than most men. Among human beings, both male and female, free relationships based upon mutual respect should be normal. On the contrary, exclusive and possessive relationships, including those based upon sexual attraction which is frequently transitory, tend to diminish the quality of living. It is desirable to minimize rather than emphasize, as we do when we think of women as a group, the relatively minor physical (and somewhat variable) physical differences between the male and the female human. We have reason to be glad that the difference exists because it gives rise to much pleasure and is a notable enrichment of life as well as the means of its continuation. It is worth noting at this stage that there is far more difference in the human condition and the social and economic problems of living as between a primitive community and a modern city, between the illiterate and the sophisticated, than there is between men and women as such in either of these situations. There is an archetypal immaturity about the boy who thinks 'all girls are silly' because he is thinking in the primitive herd way, with the gang mentality; but a great deal of this immaturity tends to spill over into adult life and is evident in race prejudice and such beliefs as that women are inferior. Thinking of human beings in categories is immature, childish. Caring about them as individuals is more difficult.

Most human beings have a natural desire to mate with an individual of the other sex and it is significant that at this stage, commonly called being in love, the individuality of the chosen or desired partner is intensified. It has to be that one, unique person who by isolation of his or her individuality seems to glow with a special splendour. During the courting period the mutual awareness of individuality seems to cocoon the lovers so that they can feel almost invisible to the rest of the world. It is easy to laugh at this, but it might be wiser to recognize in love an indication that we could all live on a much more enlightened level than we do.

The conventional outcome of love and the need to mate

is marriage which is the principal social institution by means of which the next generation is reared and the human race is continued. It would be inappropriate here to attempt to lay down guide lines for married life, but some consideration of the institution of marriage is necessary because it forms the basis of family life and is guarded by a great deal of legislation and customary restriction which affects individual freedom.

The principal advantage claimed, and rightly claimed for family life is that it provides a good way of bringing up children, and as such it is very important indeed, because bringing up the next generation is one of the principal functions of mankind and his faith in himself is founded on continuity of his species. But what do we require of family life in this respect?

Firstly, it should be stable over a sufficient period.

Secondly, it should be warm and wise.

Thirdly, it should be just and loving.

Fourthly, it should be efficient, well informed and able to give the child sensible guidance.

Many marriages fail in some or all of these respects and working partnerships entered into in a practical and responsible spirit by two people, at an appropriate age, with love and respect of each for each as independent human beings, are likely to be far better than a union based upon passionate love and sealed by supposed divine authority at an unsuitable age and without any guarantees that the practical necessities of family life will be forthcoming.

Marriage is a serious and friendly business which must be accepted as imposing limitations upon both parties, and as such it stands a good chance of growing in love. A passionate love may or may not work out as a basis for marriage and it should be recognized that very frequently it does not.

As in many branches of our life, so in relationships between men and women, we are frustrated and impoverished by grim warnings of the consequences of situations which are created by the stupidities, ignorances and anachronisms of our present ways, many of which follow from thinking of women as a group composed of a different kind of human, and, in the opinion of many men, an inferior kind.

The consequence is economic dependence of women upon men and this is still fiercely defended in the interests of family life and the home to which it is in fact inimical. The major obstacle to the real emancipation of women, instead of the hollow sham we have at present, is the abandonment of the work standard. It would then be accepted that a mother had an income of her own and each child had an income as of right. This income would become personally disposable by the child at a suitable age; it would perhaps have to be in trust and accountable up to that age. Again the idea is far from new. It is simply adapting the custom of the former aristocracy to the generality of people and this is by no means a silly thing to try to do. The objection to the old order was that it was socially unjust but those who did enjoy a privileged life had considerable experience in making the most of it. Part of the apparatus was the settlement of income upon the wife and, at appropriate stages, upon the children. In the most noble houses, as with British royalty today, certain estates and titles devolved automatically upon the children providing them with an enviable establishment of their own.

The so-called welfare state has gone a little way, and almost unconsciously, towards this pleasant state of affairs in order-ing family life. There are maternity benefits, child allowances and so on but the administration is fantastically complex and wasteful. The whole matter needs to be looked at afresh, *in principle*, and the right of women to a separate income needs to be established. Marriage can then, and for the first time for many centuries outside the aristocracy, be a genuinely free association not sustained, if it fails, by dependence and fear and the emotional squalor of an unhappy union which is about the worst possible background for children. If we care about the quality of people we should first do what we can to see that they are healthily conceived and then assure them of decent nurture in an emotionally viable home. To achieve these objectives we need to reconsider the nature of marriage, not defend a traditional institution which has many faults in its present form. Marriage should be a free and friendly relationship not a constraint; it would then be stronger not weaker.

But should there be constraints upon marriage? Should it be a privilege of those who have, so to speak, given some proof that they are fit for it? This again used to be a sanction in high society. It created many problems which were aired in eighteenth-century novels, and led to run-away marriages and Gretna Green, but these at least had a spice of real romance about them which compares favourably with the squalid slide into marriage through failure of a contraceptive which is all too common.

Marriage should be a serious and dignified state and there probably ought to be qualifications for it. There is certainly some need to counteract the pathetic prison-bonds of teen-age friendships which frustrate the healthy development of both boys and girls at a time when their lives should be opening into flower not closing into the dim limits of a scruffy bed-sitter.

There is also the question of the right age for marriage and our present practices tend to foster marriages of equal age. We need to develop social arrangements whereby there is more mixing of age-groups. Age-group isolation is a product of immature group thinking and of the decay of social life, and it is a pity. The development of personality is favoured by friendships between people of different ages. The communication of experience and the development of wisdom are frustrated by confinement to age-groups, and there is much to be said for achieving a degree of maturity and experience before accepting family responsibilities. Anthropologically very early marriage seems to be a characteristic of primitive social organizations, and on the whole it probably tends to retard both individual and communal progress, by placing unnecessary limitations upon the individual at an age when he or she is most able to learn and improve latent capacities.

It is not appropriate here to consider in detail the multifarious problems of marriage and family in relation to society and the controls which society does undoubtedly exert over the individual. The questions to be asked are whether the controls, if necessary, are the right ones, and generally they are not. The principles on which we should think are, that the bringing up of better people should be facilitated and that this process should impose the least possible restriction upon individual freedom. This means freedom within marriage as well as outside it, in other words marriage should be as little of a restraint as possible and as much an enrichment of living as possible. Here, as in all things, legislation should be aimed at enhancing and increasing freedom. Obviously personal attitudes, such as sexual possessiveness and jealousy, need considerable adjustment and possibly treatment. We can't expect to put things right only by changing institutions; we also have to adjust ourselves and if we think that human nature can't be changed we should travel among other peoples to see how very variable it can be in such matters.

Apart from marriage, our sex-life is something we need to attend to. We are over-sexed by nature and we have an appetite which has to be controlled whether we are married or not. The sexuality of people seems to vary very greatly and it is unwise to be censorious about the behaviour of people whose feelings are bound to be exclusive to themselves and unassessable by anyone else. With this warning it may still be said that there are people for whom chastity is very easy and some for whom it is inevitable, while there are others for whom it is impossible without extreme suffering or emotional mutilation. Moralists tend to notice the consequences of these things outside marriage and ignore the private hells which can be created within marriage as at present understood.

An appetite has to be controlled or it will destroy the personality. This applies to the appetites for food, drink, sleep and likewise sex. The problem is to keep the various aspects of life in proportion, to build a balanced personality. This may involve the sacrifice of one or more aspects in order to compensate for the development to an exceptional degree of a particular talent. This is common form in athletics and in monastic religion; to some extent also in scholarship, to a large extent in art. Asceticism is the deliberate application of a discipline to oneself in order to achieve an objective or a condition of living. At the other extreme appetites do undoubtedly grow by what they feed on, by being indulged. The commonest and most obvious example is drink but it is true of other appetites and one of the things any man has to learn is restraint. To some extent all of us who are sexual have to practise restraint, whether we like it or not. The problem is often the degree of restraint and it is unfortunate that popular understanding of psychology has led to emphasis upon the dangers of repression without teaching the need for control so that people can become like cars being driven without a steering wheel.

It is commonly supposed that youth is the period of greatest sexual strain. This is not true and in fact restraint in early life is probably easier than in middle age. At any age two criteria should apply, derived from very far apart sources. Firstly there is the question of *responsibility* which is an essential attribute of the civilized man. A sexual relationship should only be entered into with a full sense of responsibility towards the other person involved. To call it love without this is hypocrisy and deceit. Secondly there is the *quality* of the relationship and here we may compare sex with drinking. One can swill down liquor until one is sodden but the civilized art of drinking consists in using discrimination and restraint. On both sides there is a need for reservation if marriage is to have anything like the sacramental quality which is claimed for it. Reservation does not mean denial: it means that it should be rescued from the casual. And if sexual intercourse is outside marriage the same criteria should apply, that it is an aspect of a sincere and generous human relationship, entered into with love and respect for personality on both sides. If this ideal is to be attained the general squalor in which sexual activity occurs needs to be enlightened by knowledge and the provision of services, particularly birth control clinics with facilities for voluntary sterilization and abortion on request. These should be provided as a service which people require, on the principle that, in a free society, each has a right of control over his own body. It is very strange that at present we accept many interferences with this right during life but there are strict rules to preserve the integrity of the dead body. We accept conditions of dirt, ignorance and brutishness in the conception of a new life but surround death of the body with reverent formalities and flowers. We need to recapture reverence and wonder for the process of sex and birth. It should be enjoyed responsibly. In all fairness, it must be said that by many people it is and we should recognize, in principle, what is already good common practice. If we could clean up and emancipate our sex-life from ignorance, prejudice and taboos the cost of the necessary services would be paid for many times over in the reduction of criminality of many kinds and the number of sub-standard human beings brought into the world would be reduced.

Many personal relationships are intimate and rewarding without any sexual component. Most friendships between men and men and women and women—what we would properly call homosexual friendships if the word had not acquired a quite specialized meaning—have no erotic component and even where sexuality does occur it is a tiny fraction of the whole relationship, as it is in heterosexual friendships and marriage. The conclusion is that human relationships as such, friendships and working partnerships, are more significant for the quality of living than sexual intercourse, which should be regarded primarily, and under suitable safeguards, as the means of continuing the species, and secondarily as a delightful aspect of friendship. The quality of sexual relationships depends upon the quality of people, and this is improving, but there are many kinds of people and there are those for whom sex cannot be much more than a physical satisfaction. There are occasions in the lives of most of us, men and women, when sex and human contact are needed for themselves and without deep emotional involvement. It would be better if we recognized this instead of sweeping it under the carpet, because a great deal of squalor, unhappiness and crime results from this failure to acknowledge the truth about people, and the insatiable appetite of governments for making them 'good' by legislation. It is an impertinence for the law to protect a sane individual against himself, but it has a duty to protect every person against exploitation or injury by another. Much of our legislation about sex is fusty and unclean and it needs to be enlightened by truth.

It would be a pity to close our consideration of mating and marriage on this note because the condition which we call being in love is beautiful and inspiring. It is for many people the highest level of *being* which they ever experience. It has engendered innumerable fine works of art as well as unselfish actions and noble achievements. The sad thing is that outside very narrow limits our society represses and disapproves of love. The institution of marriage, and the rights and duties associated with it, are the principal means of frustrating passionate love which is a flame of which we tend to be afraid. Love and marriage may well come together but we should not impoverish our lives by pretending love has to be a once-for-all experience. We should not be afraid of, nor restrained from transcending ourselves.

Adult Life

There is an obligation upon each generation to fulfil itself in the conditions of its own time and not to escape into the fantasy of fulfilment through the next generation. It is a prerequisite of a good home that it should be a partnership, in the present, between two people and the children should understand their own obligation to make their own way when their chance comes, not to mortgage their parents for their own future. Children are naturally realistic and we need to consider the harm done to them by sentimental childish literature derived from adult fantasies of childhood. Such stories are unsuitable for children and provide an excuse for sloppy attitudes among parents who wish to evade the challenge of life themselves. We should seek to live in our own generation if only in order to pass on something worth while to our children, but there are other reasons.

We live in a period when young people have a genuine grievance against older people. It is justified, not because youth is right and adults are wrong, but by the failure of so many parents to become adults. Sensible young men and women do not expect to be able to put the world to rights without the benefit of experience but they do have a right to complain of a generation of parents who have, on the whole, failed to act responsibly, and so to justify their claim to adulthood. What the next generation will do is an interesting and indeed vital question.

Adult life begins when one has achieved an understanding of what one wants to do with oneself and acquired the means to do it. It follows from this definition that the longer one can defer career decision and the better one can qualify oneself, the better the chances of achieving quality in living. Is quality worth while?

For several generations liberal opinion has insisted that all men are equal. Nobody has believed this. Throughout nature and in all the products of man's skill and thought there are degrees of excellence, there are better and worse. Though the standards of judgment vary greatly nobody really doubts that some men are better than others.[39] The claim to equality was a necessary political expedient and war cry in the battle to provide equality of *opportunity* but the outcome of this battle has been, not equality but a greater insistence upon merit as a qualification for privilege. It is all very silly and based upon our ingrained idea that our standard of living should depend upon the work we do or, for married women, and with even less justice, the work our husbands to. At the root of this evil of egalitarianism, as at the root of many other evils, is money. It is silly to suppose that the opinion of the majority, who know little or nothing about a problem, is better than the opinion of those who have devoted long hours of careful study to the same problem. Men are not equal and they vary a great deal in quality but they are all entitled to justice before the law and to a living wage within the society of which they are part. After that it should be up to the individual and Society is no proper scape-goat for failure nor has it the right to over-protect and so deprive the individual of the challenges which are necessary to the development of personality. No challenge is real unless there is an element of risk which is the real spice of life.

Some challenges are not specific to individuals but affect mankind. The response has to come from individuals acting together. Among such challenges the one which looms most ominously is the population explosion. It is the kind of problem that demands adult thinking and responsible action.

There is no possible doubt that there is a limit somewhere to the number of people the surface and indeed the subterranean and subaqueous regions of Earth can support. At the present rate of increase we have not more than a hundred years to go and by then much of what we consider to be worth while in life, and most of what we regard as beautiful upon Earth, will have been destroyed. The conclusion of the U.S. National Academy of Sciences Report as far back as 1963 on the growth of world population is inescapable. In two hundred years there will be fifty people for every one there is now and 'either the birth rate of the world must come down or the death rate must go up'[40] the consequences of believing that man's future depended upon an increase in the death rate would be terrible. Respect for life would disappear.

The problem of the population explosion is not to be shrugged off with the usual jeer at the invalidity of statistics. For the advanced nations it poses an appalling dilemma between self destruction and persuading the underdeveloped countries to curtail expansion. The humane answer seems to be to spread the message as quickly as possible that quantity means diminution of the quality of life and reinforce it with assistance in raising the standards of education and of living in the areas of too rapid expansion; but it is vain to attempt to spread a gospel which one does not practice and a measure of control upon population is an urgent need in the advanced countries if only as an example. To limit quantity without taking the opportunity to improve quality genetically would seem to be foolish and dangerous. We need to achieve many new freedoms in relationships between men and women but we shall have to accept some parallel restrictions upon the present unlimited right to breed.

Among the reasons for resisting any such restriction is the fact that the normal pattern of human living is still dominated by the breeding cycle. It might be thought that man would welcome freedom from this burden and accept gladly the challenge of reorientating his life but this is not so. Most men do not want freedom and it is a sad fact that a substantial proportion of mankind, if they are given freedom, or achieve it through the efforts of a dedicated minority, soon devise means of enslaving themselves. The very institutions which were the product of enlightenment and the means of liberation become perverted by their own membership and group mentality to reimpose servitude. (Trade unions are a good example.)

But the challenge which is avoided on one front comes in on another. With improved health the average lifetime has been lengthened by twenty years. Even with the breeding cycle there is now scope for a long middle age and it is becoming increasingly clear that this is the best part of life. Youth is being recognized again as a messy period of immaturity, insecurity and incompetence in many of the necessary techniques of living. It is a period of preparation and the truly adult attitude is to welcome maturity with its opportunities, not to look back nostalgically to youth and, sometimes, even to lose oneself in the fantasy of fulfilment through one's children which is a kind of spiritual resort to the pawnbroker. It is a symptom of immaturity in adults if they take youth too seriously. This is not to say that young people should be despised; indeed present-day adults need to learn how to carry over into mature life the un-corrupted enthusiasms, the courage and dedication of youth.

But youth is a short phase and maturity may be expected to grow over a period of thirty years or more. Within adult life, and in the context of a society which will have more and more leisure as industrial processes become automated, there would seem to be scope for a division into a predominantly active phase and a subsequent contemplative phase of living during which wisdom and awareness might be achieved. Eastern cultures and religions have much to teach us in these matters but it needs to be up-dated and freed from pre-scientific superstition, out of date imagery and the corruptions which any systematic religion or philosophy acquires over a long period of time. The mature man should be capable of achieving, over a long period of years, measured by human standards, a quality of living, a refinement of self and a degree of wisdom which is quite beyond common understanding or experience at the present time.

But to return to the present and the practicalities of living in our time. Our general aim should be to improve the quality of adult life, freed as far as possible from the restrictions of the breeding cycle. This is a big statement which implies cutting away the excuses which most people have for the poverty of their way of living. So what is a full life? What is worth living for? How do we justify ourselves to ourselves and to our children who are not only entitled to ask what sort of people we are but persistently do ask this very question?

It is commonly supposed that success measured by income, and the status symbols which money can buy, is a proper index but it is very doubtful whether many people really believe this. It is a confidence trick which we impose upon ourselves and pretend that we are the only people who are not deceived. For creative people, such as artists and some kinds of scientist, engineers and those whose work is dedicated to the care of other people, such as nurses and the best kinds of doctor, the work they do is a more convincing justification. Even this is partly illusory but it provides an indicator. All these are people who *are giving out of themselves*.

But take the example of the artist because it is more revealing and more misunderstood than that of the nurse or doctor. The artist appears to live a special kind of life which art historians are inclined to treat as a whole and we all think of an artist's *life work*. To many people he seems to be a special kind of person and rather to be envied because he is creative and makes his name through his own work. In other words, among people who worship status the artist is in a specially strong position to achieve status; moreover this can actually be measured in money and the works of art can be bought and become status symbols for the owner.

The truth about an artist's life is quite different. In the first place, to be an artist of any quality, poet, painter, composer, sculptor, architect or whatever medium he may use, he has to try very hard indeed. The greatest difficulty of his work is that no outside standard of comparison is valid beyond a certain point because his work, in each separate creation, is unique and the real standard is formed in his own mind as he works. The process is so difficult that it requires a degree of concentration, and gestation over periods of time, which markedly upset the normal balances of living. It thus becomes necessary for the artist, on the one hand, to subjugate to his work, relationships and obligations which would enrich a normal life and, on the other, *to create for other people*[41] something new, unique and valuable in the work of art. He has to appear to be extremely selfish in order to create and give. In the present condition of society this is likely to cause great stress and unhappiness to other people if those people need to make the normal emotional and practical demands upon him.

Standards are generated within the artist but works of art are judged outside by comparison with other works and by public and critics who have not been through the creative fire of bringing them into being. There is thus an inevitable time-lag before general understanding can begin to catch up with what the artist has created. Often the greatest artists are those who are least apprehensible in their own time. The more the artist has to give the less likely is it to be received with understanding.

This inevitable situation creates two abuses. The artist who is tempted by the ethos of a workaday status-conscious world can earn the rewards it has to bestow in money and adulation by playing down to it, by sacrificing himself as an artist and becoming a tradesman. The other danger is that charlatans, knowing that great art is not understood in its own time, paint nonsense in the hope that the critics may recognize them as great, which does sometimes happen.

The simple fact is that the artistic products of a great creative mind are almost inevitably misunderstood or only partially appreciated in the artist's own time and the hope of posthumous fame is rather a wan flame with which to light one's life. It certainly would not satisfy the generality of people. The true lesson to be learned from the life of a great artist is that outward symbols of status and achievement are worthless. What makes an artist tick is his faith in himself and this is, I think, the key we have been seeking.

It is no use commanding faith where there is no possibility of belief. It is no easy message for the ordinary, status conscious bourgeois, or the stick together we're all right trade-unionist, that he must live by faith in himself, because this is obviously the thing which, above all he lacks. To acquire it he has to begin by measuring up to external standards which he can respect, but these are only scaffolding for the building of a real man inside. The process must begin with the rejection of the little fiddles and dishonesties which 'everybody else does'. It must be founded upon honesty and respect for truth and it can be built up until the man begins to respect himself. This is not a matter of pride; it is something quite different, a recognition of the truth about oneself and the beginning of a strength of character which can only rest upon the basis of honesty and a sense of personal responsibility.[42]

If we look across from art to science we can see that here too fidelity to the truth is essential and much of the material progress of the last century has been a by-product of respect for truth. Many of our difficulties are due to ignorance and stupid disrespect for truth.

This is not new wisdom. A holy text upon the wall of a temple at Delphi read, *Know Thyself,* and the implication is that one should not be ashamed to know. Much of the advice in *The New Testament* amounts to very much the same thing, and the necessity for the disciples to forsake home and family (*Matthew* 19) is parallel with the nature of the artistic life as outlined above. Here also is the apparent contradiction between self and obligations to others but the answer to this seems to be that service to others will only be valuable according to the quality of one's own life. It is possible so to prostrate oneself in unselfishness that one has very little to offer out of oneself.

The lustre of art as a way of life is justified but not for the

reasons usually assumed. Ideally every life should be a work
of art and as such an island of complete integrity. Success in
life cannot possibly be measured by external achievements.
Much of what men strive for, in good faith, turns out to be
worthless. There is satisfaction in building something but
sooner or later it has to be replaced. There is no permanence
in human achievement.

> *Two vast and trunkless legs of stone*
> *Stand in the desert . . . near them on the sand*
> *Half sunk a shattered visage lies . . .*
> *And on the pedestal these words appear:*
> *'My name is Ozymandias, king of kings:*
> *Look on my works ye mighty and despair.'*
> *Nothing beside remains. Round the decay*
> *Of that colossal wreck, boundless and bare*
> *The lone and level sands stretch far away.*

Because there is something of Ozymandias in most of us
Shelley's poem is sometimes regarded as rather trite. In fact
it crystallizes, in a work of art, a truth about life which
we ignore with remarkable persistence. In the present time
we are obsessed with achievement and have no means of
coming to terms with its impermanence. Achievement is truly
a by-product of some ways of life but there is no valid external
standard by which the quality of a life may be assessed
adequately. We may get glimpses, just as we may understand
a work of art according as it 'speaks to our condition', but
the goal of adult life should be to make out of ourselves the
best man or woman which we are capable of becoming. The
better we become the less recognition we are likely to get
but as we grow older we may become aware of a respect
which does not depend upon what we have done. It depends
upon the natural respect which most human beings have,
no matter how they may corrupt it, for real quality in anything, and especially in human beings. If a man is not

respected for what he IS no other honour is worth having.

But suppose we fail. Suppose there comes a stage at which we have to say that we cannot make anything respectable of our lives? This can happen most easily if we damage our minds by drugs so that we destroy the physical mechanism upon which personality depends. Perhaps the most terrible crime anyone can commit against another is to destroy his personality and it can be done by drugs and by other means which seem to prove the existence of sheer evil. This is the sin against the spirit of man.[43] There seems to be no way out short of death.

The idea of a conscience which distinguishes between good and evil in all our doings is too naïve but we do have the power within ourselves to construct or to ruin our characters. Just as the artist has an intuition, born of the interaction between himself and what he is doing, of the standards he must achieve, and just as the scientist is aware of a standard of truth which must not be tampered with, so, in the fashioning of our lives, we have a conception of ourselves to respect, and standards of honesty to observe, if we are to achieve quality in living.

I have said that there is need for a new tenderness, for imagination, for a greater sharing of responsibility towards the future of mankind, for a new respect for quality. A good thing can become its opposite by mere increase, as we have seen throughout this book, and this applies to what we call *permissiveness*. Tolerance is not only a virtue but a necessity. At all costs we must not enforce conformity, and censorship is immoral, but the health of a society depends upon fearless expression of opinion, not upon evasion and there is need for a *new contempt* towards the shoddy, the corrupt, the pretentious and the people who seek to get more out of society than they contribute to it. We are individuals and the health of human communities depends upon our being responsible individuals of good quality, but as individuals we depend upon communal life. This is an inescapable necessity and there is a personal obligation of public generosity upon all of us.

All temporal powers are transitory and most of them generate the means of their own destruction which is often the repression of minority opinion. The forces of human will and feeling are inexorable and for some years now there has been a growing and impoverishing meanness, a concern with self and the rejection of healthy responsibility. This has been the immediate response to the imposition of social and political systems which were of temporary value and their retention beyond their useful life. The pendulum must now swing back to recognition of the inescapable fact that all organizations, and the implementation of all systems, depends upon the quality and generosity of individual men and women.

The main conclusion of this book must be that, on two accounts, we need to cultivate quality; firstly because no society of human beings can remain competitive for long if it does not develop and foster quality rather than mediocrity in its people, and secondly because happiness is related to man's ability to feel that he is fulfilling himself—getting somewhere as we say—not merely vegetating; and although vegetable people may often be pleasant and good friends we all know instinctively that there is a need to try.

It should not, however, be thought that only the most talented, educated and excellent people are worth while and capable of living fine lives, because this is patently untrue. The community of human beings requires an infinite variety of talents at many levels. We are all different and happiness and quality in our individual lives, and the accumulating morale and sense of achievement of the community, come from each person trying to make the most of his own gifts and being free to do so. The enemies are apathy and laziness.

It is not a question of making the most profit or doing minimum work for maximum pay (which is basically the same attitude). What we need for our *well being* is to feel personally involved in what we are doing, work or activity, paid or unpaid, at whatever level, from routine maintenance such as cleaning windows to creative thinking in science or philosophy. To be well we need to do as well as we can, but always remembering that the integrity and quality of being is what matters; activity—what we do—is a means to that end.

Whether we like it or not, and whatever social theories or ideals we may uphold, human beings do differentiate themselves and it seems that there is a new differentiation pattern emerging and cutting right across the old patterns of class which are becoming irrelevant. It is a differentiation between *those who live actively* and *those who are content to exist*.

In the past, aristocracies have been formed by conquest, by exploitation and in many cases by superior ability and energy. Wealth has moved from the governed to the governors and the moulds of class distinction have been formed. Some dynasties have maintained their position over many generations but none have been permanent. Some good institutions have been corrupted by the growth of power and others have withered away from lack of strength. In our era of revolution something nearer to equilibrium has been achieved, nearer to equality than man has been for a long time, despite the manifold and obvious inequalities which remain between people, and between peoples according to their degree of development. But the impetus of the levelling process has diminished and no longer inspires the more advanced peoples though it still matters a great deal in backward countries.

We are at a new parting of the ways. One leads to a new form of differentiation by power and the fresh concentration of wealth in a governing minority of the old type (possibly a bureauracy) which would, because of what has happened in human thought during the last hundred years probably collapse into war, revolution and the suicide of the human race. The other way could lead to the improvement of man-

kind and the achievement of standards which we cannot forsee, but it would be foolish to suppose that this path, the
way which the argument of this book has indicated, would
not be fraught with difficulty and agonizing problems.

It is not in the nature of man to succeed by taking the
easier path. Mankind needs the stimulus of difficulty. We cannot stop trying without degenerating but we have to have
an idea of where we are going and belief that it is worth
the effort. By the nature of man the goal cannot be for
long the levelling of egalitarianism. The alternative is now
to use what we have partially achieved through the social
changes of the last century and a half, as a basis for believing
that man is now ready to improve *himself*. It will then be for
better men and women than ourselves to solve the next
round of problems.

NOTES

NOTES ON THE TEXT

1. See *Sex, Science and Society*, by A. S. Parkes, Oriel Press, Newcastle, 1967. (p. 21)

2. This is a reminder that the commandment, not to commit adultery, refers to an offence against a man's right to have only his own children by his wife and was not a prohibition of extra-marital intercourse which was commonplace in a slave-owning patriarchal society. The law was clearly intended to ensure that children by a slave would also be his own. (p. 23)

3. Parkes, *op. cit.* (note 1.) (p. 23)

4. George Fox, *Epistle No. 150*, 1657. See also L. Hugh Doncaster *God in Every Man*, Allen and Unwin, London, 1963. (p. 25)

5. In the case of identical twins uniqueness is acquired in the process of development after birth. Each has, and responds to different experiences. (p. 27)

6. Winston Churchill in World War II. (p. 29)

7. A profound study of this danger is *Grey Eminence*, by Aldous Huxley, Chatto & Windus, 1941. (p. 30)

8. People get the police force which the average deserve and this can be very hard on the creative minority and upon the young. (p. 40)

9. As Rudolf Schwartz has pointed out (*Sunday Times*, December 1968) women have a great potential advantage over men in this respect. (p. 48)

10. A curious side effect at present is an actual shortage of skilled labour in some places but this economic difficulty should not obscure the main problem. As population increases there may well be shortages of skilled people and if the growth leads to lower educational standards, as seems likely, the shortage may be accentuated to the point of disaster when there are huge numbers of unskilled people and not enough with the knowledge to maintain production of necessities. (p. 54)

11. See *The Rise of Meritocracy*, by Michael Young, Thames and Hudson, London, 1958. (p. 56)

12. Ironically the most advanced socialist communities are the most ruthless investors in capital equipment. (p. 59)

13. It is made more, not less likely by the population explosion. (See note 10 above.) (p. 59)

14. This surely is the test of belief in equality—the willingness to share with the poor. The comfortable and somewhat hypocritical argument that the poor must be made rich is an evasion. (p. 62)

15. Most higher incomes are not based on work and popular egalitarian thinking regards this as an evil. If the work-standard were abandoned the problem of excessive riches

would have to be considered from a quite different point of view. (p. 63)

16. This is reflected in the quality of our architecture, especially in Britain. (p. 63)

17. There would also be an enormous saving in the administration of the social services which are a heavy burden and produce a great deal of unnecessary work. It is a sympton of the disease which is crippling Britain, and other countries, that this useless work is actually welcomed and cities offer special inducements to government departments to bring such useless work into their area in order to 'create employment'. (p. 64)

18. It will probably appear to historians in the future (if there is a future in which history can be studied) that just as Britain was the pioneer of the industrial revolution so it was also, in the second half of the twentieth century, the first country to get into such a mess as a result of industrialism that it had to change direction. What now appears to be decadence in Britain may, and probably will, look like the creative transition towards a better way of life. (p. 69)

19. Mythology is a valuable technique of generalizing the problems of living. We should cultivate it. (p. 71)

20. Robert Bridges:

> *'I too will something make*
> *And joy in the making'* (p.73)

21. *'Top of the Pops'* is a symptom of the work syndrome. (p. 74)

22. In this chapter the capital letter G is used convention-

ally for God as understood by Christians. The convention is discussed in the third paragraph of the next chapter. (p. 77)

23. 'Cogito, ergo sum' (I think, therefore I am) *Le Discours de la Méthode*, by René Descartes (1596-1650). (p. 89)

24. *The Phenomenon of Man*, by Taillard de Chardin, Collins, London, 1959. (p. 90)

25. *Sex, Science and Society*, by A. S. Parkes, Oriel Press, Newcastle, 1967. (p. 90)

26. This is not, of course, the peculiarity of modern man: consider Socrates. It should be a sobering thought that only the best modern minds are on the level of the best minds of 2,500 years ago. (p. 91)

27. *Politics* 1.2. (p. 94)

28. An American presidential election is perhaps the most spectacular example of politics reduced to farce. No one seems to ask effectively whether all this nonsense is not a certain means of excluding any candidate who could possibly be suitable on grounds of intellect or integrity. (p. 100)

29. Darwin merely confirmed and explained this in his theory of evolution. He did not invent it. (p. 103)

30. Probably, J. Reading (1677-1764). (p. 106)

31. In defiance of ordinary arithmetic as taught, the sum consists of the whole of each of the parts *plus* the relationship between them and the different relationship of the sum to its environment by virtue of its being the sum and not two separate parts. Thus in terms of relationships and qualities $1 + 1 = 2 + x + y$. (p. 109)

32. An *epiphenomenon* is something that happens in addition to something else, not on its own. (p. 112)

33. It seems to be an axiom of the civil service that individuality must be suppressed within the service. There must be a sacrifice of personality to 'the service'. This is probably good and necessary but it means that civil servants tend to be occupationally prejudiced against individuality and originality. (p. 114)

34. I have found it useful here to accept the discipline of the sonnet form rather than try to express these ideas in prose. In the course of my studies for this book I have made many drawings, paintings, written poems and two novels, all of which are unpublished. They have been part of the process of discovery. (Preface and p. 119)

35. But see also page 134 *et seq.* (p. 120)

36. And by parsimony. (p. 127)

37. Some of the criticism and resentment of examinations stems from the current tendency to over-protect. (p. 129)

38. In return the more developed countries could offer free higher education to Greenlanders, Norwegians, etc. (p. 129)

39. George Orwell's wry comment that 'some are more equal than others' derives from the social obsessions of his time. Equality is *not* an ideal. It would be a disaster and could only be achieved if we were all born from a single sub-divided egg. Even then the identical creatures would be differentiated 'unfairly' by the accidents of environment and experience as happens to identical twins. (p. 143)

40. *Sex, Science and Society*, by A. S. Parkes (see Note 1). (p. 144)

41. It is commonly supposed, especially by would-be artists, that an artist works for himself but, though there is an element of self-discovery and self-fulfilment in art, as in any other kind of activity, the artist must communicate if it is only with one other human being or with a supposed audience which, in the case of a very original work, may have to be in the future. Art is, in essence, completely unselfish. (p. 147)

42. One of the great delusions is that one can absolve oneself from personal responsibility by being loyal to a group whose general aims one approves. (p. 148)

43. Or, in religious terms, the sin against the Holy Spirit. What is cynically called 'brain washing' is in this category. (p. 150)